Spelling Workbook

Belongs To:

_____

Copyright © 2023 Newbee Publication

ALL RIGHTS RESERVED

This book may not be reproduced or transmitted in any form or by any means, electronic or mechanical, without written permission from the author.

Thanks for Purchase
Scan QR code for more publications

Word Cloud

How to use this Spelling Workbook

If you're looking to improve your spelling skills, this practice workbook is a great resource. The first lesson includes instructions and examples. To make the most of your practice time, here are some tips to keep in mind:

- Only practice when you're feeling focused and ready to learn.
- Take your time with each exercise and avoid trying to complete the entire lesson in one sitting.
- Use a dictionary to look up word meanings rather than using digital tools.
- Keep track of any words you struggle with and make a point of practicing them more frequently.
- Try incorporating new words into your writing and speech to help reinforce your learning.
- Regularly review the words you've learned to help cement them in your long-term memory.
- Don't hesitate to ask for help if you're having difficulty with a particular word or concept.
- Lastly, celebrate your progress and accomplishments along the way to help keep yourself motivated and engaged.
- You can photocopy pages to practice again or consider purchasing another workbook once you've finished.

Making learning process easy by simplifying complex information and breaking it down into manageable chunks

Any big words; you can chunk them into two or three words. Using chunking and associating the word with a vivid and heartwarming image can help children remember and comprehend the words
for example:-

Measure: Me - a - sure or "Mea - sure"
Sounds like "May sure." Imagine a person taking measurements with a tape measure, ensuring that everything is accurately sized and "may sure" of the dimensions.

Motion: "Mo- ti - on" or Mo - tion
sounds like "Ocean." Visualize yourself surfing on ocean waves, experiencing the motion.

Dialect: "Di - a - lect" or Di - alect
Sounds like "Die Elect." Imagine a funny scenario where all the electricity suddenly disappears, and people start speaking in different funny accents, causing confusion and laughter. This is how you can remember "dialect" by connecting it with "die elect" and the humorous situation of language change without electricity.

Innocence: "In - no - cence" or In - nocence
Sounds like "Innocent." Visualize a young child (innocent) playing with a fluffy little bunny, smiling and full of wonder. The child's innocence is reflected in their pure and gentle interactions with the bunny.

Knowledge: "Know - ledge" or Know - ledge
Sounds like "Know the edge." Imagine standing on the edge of a cliff, looking out at the vast horizon, eager to learn and understand everything that lies ahead. The edge represents the boundary of what you know and what you want to explore, symbolizing the pursuit of knowledge.

Lesson 1

Re-write Words

Abstract	ABSTRACT		
Applause			
Began			
Believe			
Critic			
Cliché			

Find Letters

Abstract	M g(a)p s(b)m(s)d g j(t)a p r k s(a)p i(c)x o p(t)
Applause	g(a)o j n b p m p u l b p a t s r u l s o j a v r e
Began	z w m B i e k a n h d s g u e a b r n k o a j t w
Believe	l k j i B l n d m e s l k r i q w e d i v y e h g d
Critic	a b d l C d g r o l p t i n g h t q x i f h n c j k
Cliché	b p s C m k l q o n i f j c d l h a u r t f d l e p

These mnemonics create memorable phrases or sentences that help you recall the words easier. You can also create your own mnemonics based on personal associations or stories to better remember these words.

Abstract:
Mnemonic: "A Butterfly Soars Through Rainbows, Engaging Creative Thoughts."

Applause:
Mnemonic: "All People Praise Loudly After Unbelievable Spectacular Events."

Began:
Mnemonic: "Birds Eagerly Greeted A New day."

Believe:
Mnemonic: "Beyond Every Lie, I Ever Expected Valid Evidence."

Critic:
Mnemonic: "Cats Roar In Theatres, Irate and Critical."

Cliché:
Mnemonic: "Clever Lions In Cozy Houses, Enjoying."

Find Meanings from Dictionary and write them here

Abstract _____

Applause _____

Began _____

Believe _____

Critic _____

Cliché _____

Write out these words in Capital letters

abstract _____

applause _____

began _____

believe _____

critic _____

cliché _____

Across
5. A concept or idea that is not concrete or easily defined.
6. To have faith or trust in something or someone.

Down
1. An overused expression or idea that has lost its originality or impact.
2. The sound of clapping hands to show appreciation or approval.
3. A person who analyzes and evaluates works of art, literature, or performances.
4. Started or initiated an action or process.

Write out the Synonyms and Antonyms of these words

	Synonyms	Antonyms
Abstract		
Applause		
Began		
Believe		
Critic		
Cliché		

Match the Unscramble Words

Abstract	leveieb	....
Applause	éichcl	....
Began	critic	....
Believe	pslepaau	....
Critic	ebang	....
Cliché	ttcsbraa	......Abstract..............

Fill the blanks and Make the sentences using above words

1. It has become a __Cliché__ to say that Prague is the most beautiful city in Europe.

2. The audience _____ clapping and cheering.

3. Sheila got a round of __Applause__ when she finished.

4. You have to _____ in yourself. That's the secret of success.

5. Mr Masack is an outspoken _____ of the present government.

6. Modern __Abstract__ art is outside my province.

Match the words to the shape

Abstract, Applause, Began, Believe, Critic, Cliché

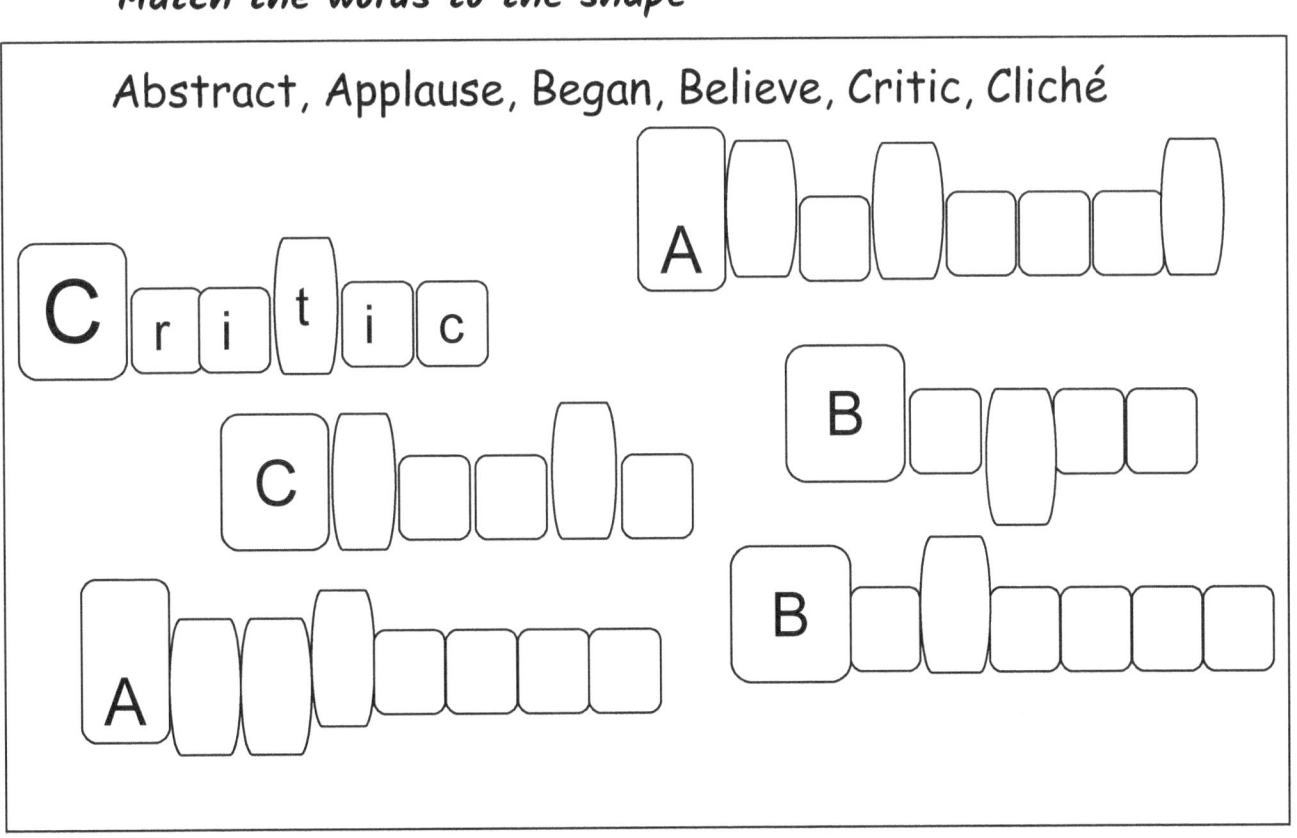

Wordsearch
Puzzle #1

```
E C X P W L J N S Z X W W S H B
I Q B B Y R G X G Q Y H U W E F
A X O V Q K D F U U Z O B S I A
J B D N H X B B I E K H U T G G
B H S G A Z N D K A E A Z W J Q
G N P T G X V Y M Z L R L W O P
N B P T R O U L Y P U X P P H N
K E C F F A S A P C U J A K K N
N G V L V R C A U R R L H C X
R A K L I R F T F I V K E U U O
L N X Q U C U R H T F L I P L I
K K U L B H H Z D I J G P E Y L
Y A N V C O L V J C Y P U P B N
F C S D O J G U N M G E Q R B S
G D S H K G N C I C W A Y C Z M
M Y S K I X W H B E L I E V E S
```

ABSTRACT   APPLAUSE
BEGAN   BELIEVE
CLICHÉ   CRITIC

What rhymes with these words

Abstract — Coapt, intact, interact, adapt

Applause — Cause, claws, jaws, laws, pause

Began — _____

Believe — _____

Critic — _____

Cliché — _____

Find hidden words

Abstract — _____

Applause — Use, Sale, Pal Apple, Pule, Lap

Began — _____

Believe — _____

Critic — It, Tic, Crit

Cliché — _____

Lesson 2

Re-write Words

Abroad			
Aloud			
Bias			
Busy			
Chorus			
Column			

Find Letters

Abroad	M g A p s b m s d g j r p o k s a p i t x o p d l n
Aloud	g r o j n b A m q u l b p c t s r w l o j a u r e k d
Bias	z w m B i e k a n h d s r u e c b r m k o a j t w i
Busy	L k j i B l n d m u l k r o s w t d i x y e h g d n t
Chorus	A b d l C d g i l h t s n g o t q r e f h u c j s r t
Column	B p s C m k l q o n e f j c d l h a u r t m d l e n p

Find Meanings from Dictionary and write them here

Abroad _____

Aloud   _____

Bias   _____

Busy   _____

Chorus _____

Column _____

Write out these words in Capital letters

abroad _____

aloud   _____

bias   _____

busy   _____

chorus _____

column _____

These mnemonics create memorable phrases or sentences that help you recall the words easier. You can also create your own mnemonics based on personal associations or stories to better remember these words.

Abroad:
Mnemonic: "A Bee Ran Over A Desert."

Aloud:
Mnemonic: "A Loud Owl Understood Differently."

Bias:
Mnemonic: "Being Aware Influences our Sight."

Busy:
Mnemonic: "Bunnies Usually Seem Yippy."

Chorus:
Mnemonic: "Children Harmonize Often, Rejoicing Under Stars."

Column:
Mnemonic: "Careful Owls Landed Upon Majestic Nests."

Write out the Synonyms and Antonyms of these words

	Synonyms	Antonyms
Abroad		
Aloud		
Bias		
Busy		
Chorus		
Column		

Match the Unscramble Words

Abroad	sybu	....
Aloud	uonmCl	....
Bias	obaard	....
Busy	uaold	....
Chocus	isab	....
Column	shccou	....

Across

2. Occupied with or engaged in activity or work.
3. In or to a foreign country or place.
4. A vertical division or section in a written or printed work.

Down

1. A group of singers or voices that perform together.
2. Prejudice or inclination in favour of or against something.
3. Spoken or uttered with audible volume.

Fill the blanks and Make the sentences using above words

1. She writes a regular _____ for a national newspaper.

2. I heard him suddenly laugh _____.

3. The committee are _____ laying down a general policy.

4. Your plan of going _____ is an audacious decision.

5. The proposal was greeted with a _____ of approval.

6. Students were evaluated without _____ or favoritism.

Match the words to the shape

Abroad, Aloud, Bias, Busy, Chorus, Column

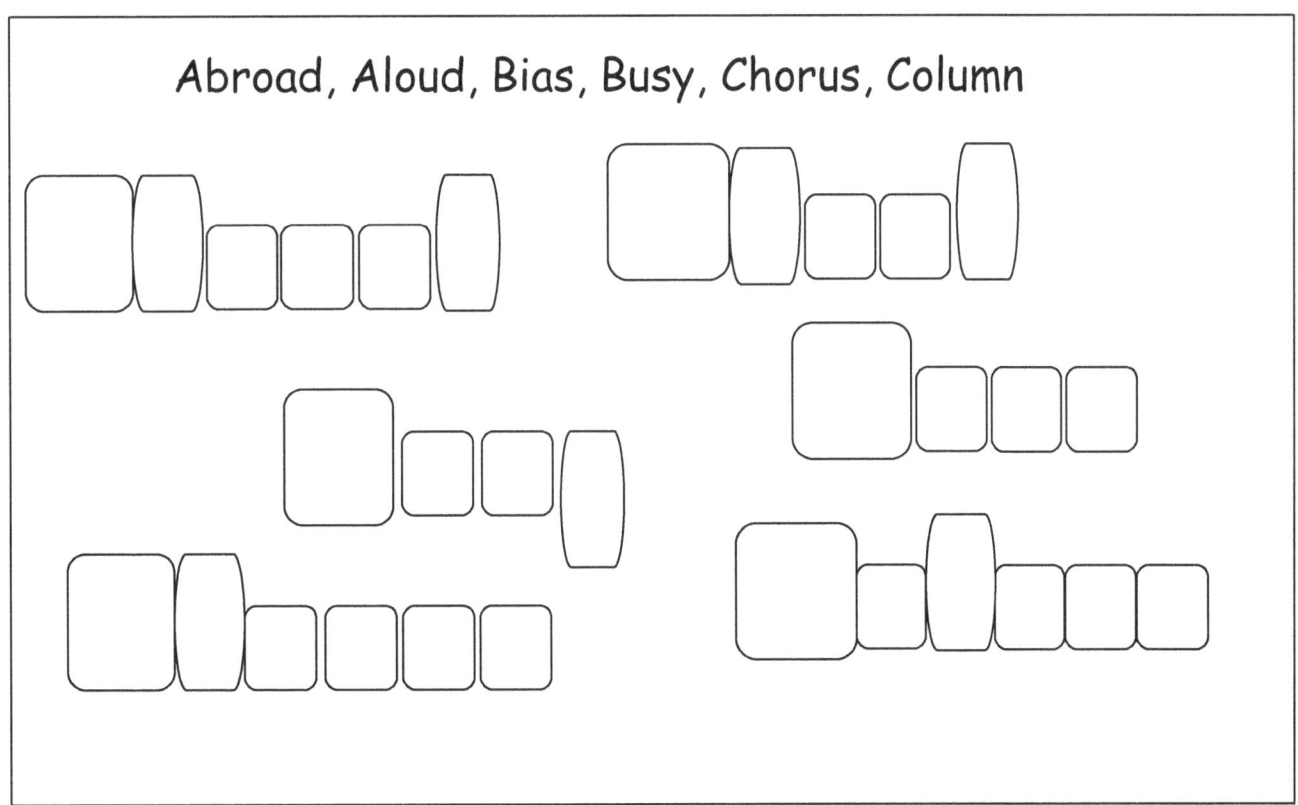

Wordsearch

Puzzle # 2

```
S E Y R X Q M Y G I J R Y I N L
W Q U X K Z S P F Q H N J W W I
V A B R O A D A T Y E A E X Q P
J A N X W U E O C Y S R Q I R D
D T N N P Y Y G S H W Y F J F F
F N U Z G F Y U M V O P N Y K W
E Q B K N Y B A R B V R X J F Q
E D L X D Q A L U O Q X U I R R
P X Z H X M L R Y C B L S S M R
X K C D K U O B U C O C Y C Z Q
Z P Z A Z F U I U X O L W X P N
A Q K T C I D A Q I V C U Z H Z
I Y X T V C W S O S T I U M N R
V Y U O U B N T Y Q Y A L K N O
X E I V E V S O P S N O L P A Y
N F U G L P O Q B D W Q C W J M
```

ABROAD ALOUD
BIAS BUSY
CHORUS COLUMN

What rhymes with these words

Abroad　　_____

Aloud　　 _____

Bias　　　_____

Busy　　　_____

Chorus　　_____

Column　　_____

Find hidden words

Abroad　　_____

Aloud　　 _____

Bias　　　_____

Busy　　　_____

Chorus　　_____

Column　　_____

Lesson 3

Re-write Words

Boast			
Boost			
Chef			
Chief			
Direct			
Dialect			

Find Letters

Boast	M g A p s b m s d g j r p o k s a p i s x o p d t n
Boost	g r o j n b A m q u o b p c t r w l o j a s r e k d t
Chef	z w m c i e k a n h d s r u e c b r m f o a j t w i
Chief	L k j i c l n h m u l k r o i s w t d e x y e h f d n t
Direct	A b d l c d g i l h t r n g o t q r e f h u c j s r t
Dialect	B p s d m k i q o n a f j c d l h e u r c m d t e n p

Find Meanings from Dictionary and write them here

Boast _____

Boost _____

Chef _____

Chief _____

Direct _____

Dialect _____

Write out these words in Capital letters

boast _____

boost _____

chef _____

chief _____

direct _____

dialect _____

These mnemonics create memorable phrases or sentences that help you recall the words easier. You can also create your own mnemonics based on personal associations or stories to better remember these words.

Boast:
Mnemonic: "Bold Owls Always Show Triumph."

Boost:
Mnemonic: "Brilliant Opportunities Offer Support Today."

Chef:
Mnemonic: "Cooking Has Exquisite Flavors."

Chief:
Mnemonic: "Courageous Hawks In Eagle Feathers."

Direct:
Mnemonic: "Drive In Right, Ensure Correct Turns."

Dialect:
Mnemonic: "Diverse Individuals Adapt, Learn, Embrace Cultural Tones."

Write out the Synonyms and Antonyms of these words

	Synonyms	Antonyms
Boast		
Boost		
Chef		
Chief		
Direct		
Dialect		

Match the Unscramble Words

Boast	citdre	....
Boost	Hiecf	....
Chef	cdeital	....
Chief	ostbo	....
Direct	cehf	....
Dialect	tasbo	....

Across

3. A particular form of language spoken in a specific region or community.

5. The leader or highest-ranking person in an organization or group.

6. To brag or speak proudly about one's achievements.

Down

1. To increase or improve something, often in a significant way.

2. To give clear and precise instructions or guidance.

4. A professional cook who is skilled in preparing meals.

Fill the blanks and Make the sentences using above words

1. He couldn't help but _____ about his new car's top speed.

2. The new marketing campaign is expected to _____ sales by 30%.

3. The _____ prepared a mouthwatering gourmet meal for the guests.

4. The _____ of the tribe was known for his wisdom and guidance.

5. Could you _____ me to the nearest gas station?

6. The locals spoke a unique _____ that was distinct from the neighboring regions.

Match the words to the shape

Boast, Boost, Chef, Chief, Direct, Dialect

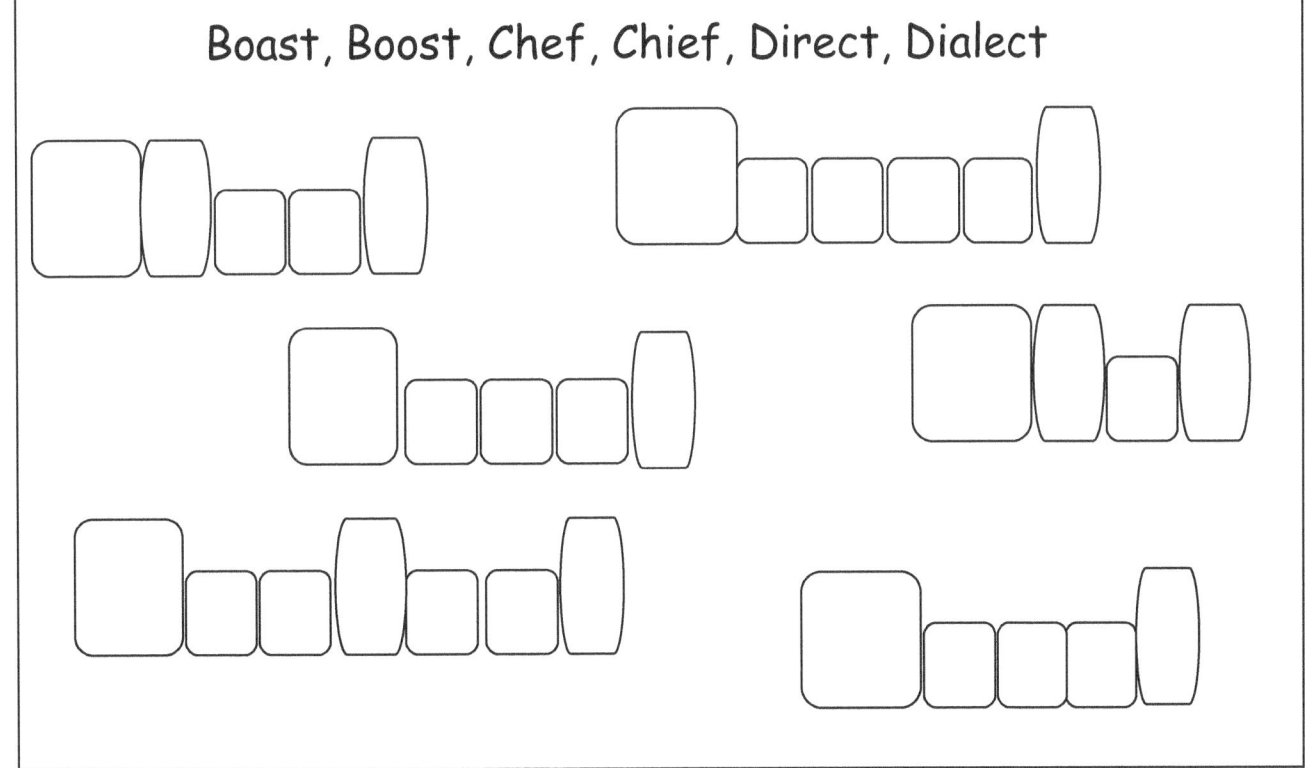

Wordsearch
Puzzle # 3

```
o y x a t m i a m a n j t s f w
k j i q o f y b p c a v l k o y
v y u e f r z b o i l b z e r d
w c t m n h v i a a o p x e q d
r h e k d b r b y x s i o k t i
o i u e l k b s o p z t x t y c
w e x s d b r g x o t w t k u w
w f t d s m e r v g s f t k l d
v o i i g w a v c g z t z s u i
v s z a o i r u q a x d l j s r
b i d l f k z b t d x f o v w p
f j q e a x x h d y g b e l l i
g e z c p q l x z s j e d u d e
v v y t i p c w y a v t x d m y
p d i r e c t s h t q u c h e f
d x q h g q x e i f x f k z t k
```

BOAST BOOST
CHEF CHIEF
DIALECT DIRECT

What rhymes with these words

Boast _____

Boost _____

Chef _____

Chief _____

Direct _____

Dialect _____

Find hidden words

Boast _____

Boost _____

Chef _____

Chief _____

Direct _____

Dialect _____

Reading Comprehension

Please read the passage, and as you do, underline the words you have learned in this lesson. Afterward, answer the questions provided.

Title: The Culinary Contest

In a bustling city, a prestigious culinary contest was underway, attracting the most skilled chefs from all around. The contestants were eager to boast about their culinary prowess and hoped to boost their careers with a victory.

Among the participants was Chef Marcus, a seasoned chef known for his innovative dishes. He had been the chief chef at a renowned restaurant for years and was determined to showcase his talents at the contest. Chef Marcus was excited to be competing against other chefs with diverse backgrounds and cooking styles.

The judges, a panel of direct and honest food critics, were ready to evaluate each dish carefully. They looked forward to tasting a wide variety of dishes, each prepared with unique ingredients and cooking techniques. The dialect of flavors and aromas in the air filled the room, making everyone's mouths water in anticipation.

As the contest progressed, Chef Marcus presented his signature dish—a delectable fusion of cultural flavors. He spoke aloud about the inspiration behind the dish, explaining how he wanted to create a harmonious chorus of tastes that would delight the taste buds. The judges listened attentively, intrigued by the story behind the creation of the dish.

After a fierce competition, the judges had a challenging decision to make. Each dish had its own merits, and it was tough to choose a winner. They carefully considered the taste, presentation, and creativity of each chef's offering.

Finally, the judges reached a consensus, and Chef Marcus emerged as the winner of the culinary contest. His clever use of ingredients and masterful combination of flavors impressed the judges, making him the new culinary champion.

Reading Comprehension Questions:

1. What was the purpose of the culinary contest?

2. How did Chef Marcus plan to impress the judges with his dish?

3. What did the judges consider when evaluating the dishes?

4. Why did Chef Marcus become the winner of the contest?

Lesson 4

Re-write Words

Dispatch			
Display			
Exchange			
Enough			
Future			
Futile			

Find Letters

Dispatch	m g d p d c m i g j s p k a t p i u c a m d h e
Display	g r o j n c d o q u i b s c r n p t o i l b a y e d
Exchange	z w e d b x k a n g c u h e a r g k n a g l w e
Enough	l k j i e l n i m o a k u p m e l g o r e h y e d
Future	a f d l u d g r l f q t n c u q i o f r n j s e t i
Futile	b p s f m k l x o u e f t n d c i a u c m o l i n e

These mnemonics are designed to create memorable associations or phrases that can help you remember the words better. Feel free to modify them or come up with your own mnemonics based on what helps you remember most effectively!

Dispatch:
Mnemonic: "Donkeys Easily Send Pigeons And Carry Helpful Communications."

Display:
Mnemonic: "Dancing Performers Light Up Spectacular Lights And Yell."

Exchange:
Mnemonic: "Eagles X-ray Cars, Horses, And New Gems, Eventually."

Enough:
Mnemonic: "Eager Night Owls Understand Gratitude, Hear."

Future:
Mnemonic: "Frogs Usually Take Unfamiliar Trails, Eventually Reaching."

Futile:
Mnemonic: "Fierce Unicorns Tried Inventing Ladders, Earning."

Find Meanings from Dictionary and write them here

Dispatch _____

Display   _____

Exchange _____

Enough   _____

Future   _____

Futile   _____

Write out these words in Capital letters

dispatch _____

display   _____

exchange _____

enough   _____

future   _____

futile   _____

Write out the Synonyms and Antonyms of these words

	Synonyms	Antonyms
Dispatch		
Display		
Exchange		
Enough		
Future		
Futile		

Match the Unscramble Words

Dispatch	gchnexae	....
Display	letfiu	....
Exchange	turfeu	....
Enough	atipschd	....
Future	ydaispl	....
Futile	nhuoeg	....

Fill the blanks and Make the sentences using above words

1. The latest _____ was held up for three hours at the border.

2. He mustered up_____ courage to attack the difficulty.

3. The president described these activities as _____.

4. The climax of the Carnival celebration was a firework_____.

5. Conor is very optimistic about the _____.

6. Euro is expected to fall in the foreign _____ markets.

Match the words to the shape

Dispatch, Display, Exchange, Enough, Future, Futile

Wordsearch
Puzzle # 4

```
L P P O V Q L D C K Q N F Z I O
O H F S E X C H A N G E W G Q A
Z W F G U A Z K Q Q F H K I I W
N V W S Y V R J W E Z W X E L M
M N V A J Z L P L U Y V G P H N
R Z W I K W E I A D L Z H H T K
S W K T J R T C W Z P S U Y U N
R B V V U U Z G J N W B A I I G
T S A T F M H D J B F L Y P O Z
R A U V E J Y G H T P S U D V C
D F S A Q H G G K S O M Q H C I
J I R M V Q U K I P Z D X F Q A
J G U G S O I D I J Z V M M M V
B J M I N E D I S P A T C H A Z
H S K E H H L N L R F J Y C V F
T P J D S I U L P W K T F G Z F
```

DISPATCH DISPLAY
ENOUGH   EXCHANGE
FUTILE   FUTURE

What rhymes with these words

Dispatch _____

Display _____

Exchange _____

Enough _____

Future _____

Futile _____

Find hidden words

Dispatch _____

Display _____

Exchange _____

Enough _____

Future _____

Futile _____

Across

5. The act of sending something or someone to a specific destination.

6. The act of giving one thing and receiving another in return.

Down

1. A sufficient quantity or degree of something.

2. The time or period that will come after the present.

3. To exhibit or show something for others to see.

4. Having no useful result or effect; pointless or ineffective.

Lesson 5

Re-write Words

Fatigue			
Federal			
Generous			
Genetic			
Genius			
Genuine			

Find Letters

Fatigue	m g A f d c m i g j s p k a t p i u c g m d u h e k
Federal	g f o j n e d o q u i d s e n p t o i l b r a y e d m
Generous	z w g d b e k a n c u h e a r g o n a u l w e f g s
Genetic	g k j i e l n i m o a k u p m e l g o t e h y i d c e
Genius	a f d l u d g r l f e t n c u q i o f u r n j s e t i m
Genuine	b p s m g l o u e f t n d u c i a c n m o l i e f p s

These mnemonics are designed to create memorable associations or phrases that can help you remember the words better. Feel free to modify them or come up with your own mnemonics based on what helps you remember most effectively!

Fatigue:
Mnemonic: "Feeling Always Tired, I Get Up Early."

Federal:
Mnemonic: "Frogs Eagerly Dance, Eating Ripe Apples Lying."

Generous:
Mnemonic: "Good Elephants Never Expect Rewards; Others Understand Sharing."

Genetic:
Mnemonic: "Genies Easily Navigate The Interesting Code."

Genius:
Mnemonic: "Great Eagles Nurture Ideas, Unlocking Success."

Genuine:
Mnemonic: "Giraffes Exude Niceness, Understanding Inherent Empathy."

Find Meanings from Dictionary and write them here

Fatigue _____

Federal _____

Generous _____

Genetic _____

Genius _____

Genuine _____

Write out these words in Capital letters

fatigue _____

federal _____

generous _____

genetic _____

genius _____

genuine _____

Write out the Synonyms and Antonyms of these words

	Synonyms	Antonyms
Fatigue		
Federal		
Generous		
Genetic		
Genius		
Genuine		

Match the Unscramble Words

Fatigue	nuegeni	....
Federal	tieegcn	....
Generous	tefigua	....
Genetic	senugi	....
Genius	dflerea	....
Genuine	deafrle	....

Fill the blanks and Make the sentences using above words

1. After a long day of work, I felt extreme _____ and could barely keep my eyes open.
2. The _____ government implemented new policies to address the economic challenges.
3. She has a _____ heart and is always willing to help those in need.
4. The doctor explained that the patient's condition was caused by a _____ predisposition.
5. Albert Einstein was a scientific _____ who revolutionized the field of physics.
6. I could sense his _____ concern for my well-being as he offered me sincere advice.

Match the words to the shape

Fatigue, Federal, Generous, Genetic, Genius, Genuine

Across

3. Authentic, real, or sincere.
4. A person with exceptional intellectual or creative abilities. (Genius)
6. Pertaining to the national government of a country.

Down

1. Extreme tiredness or exhaustion.
2. Relating to traits or characteristics passed down from parents to offspring.
5. Showing a willingness to give or share; not selfish.

Wordsearch
Puzzle # 5

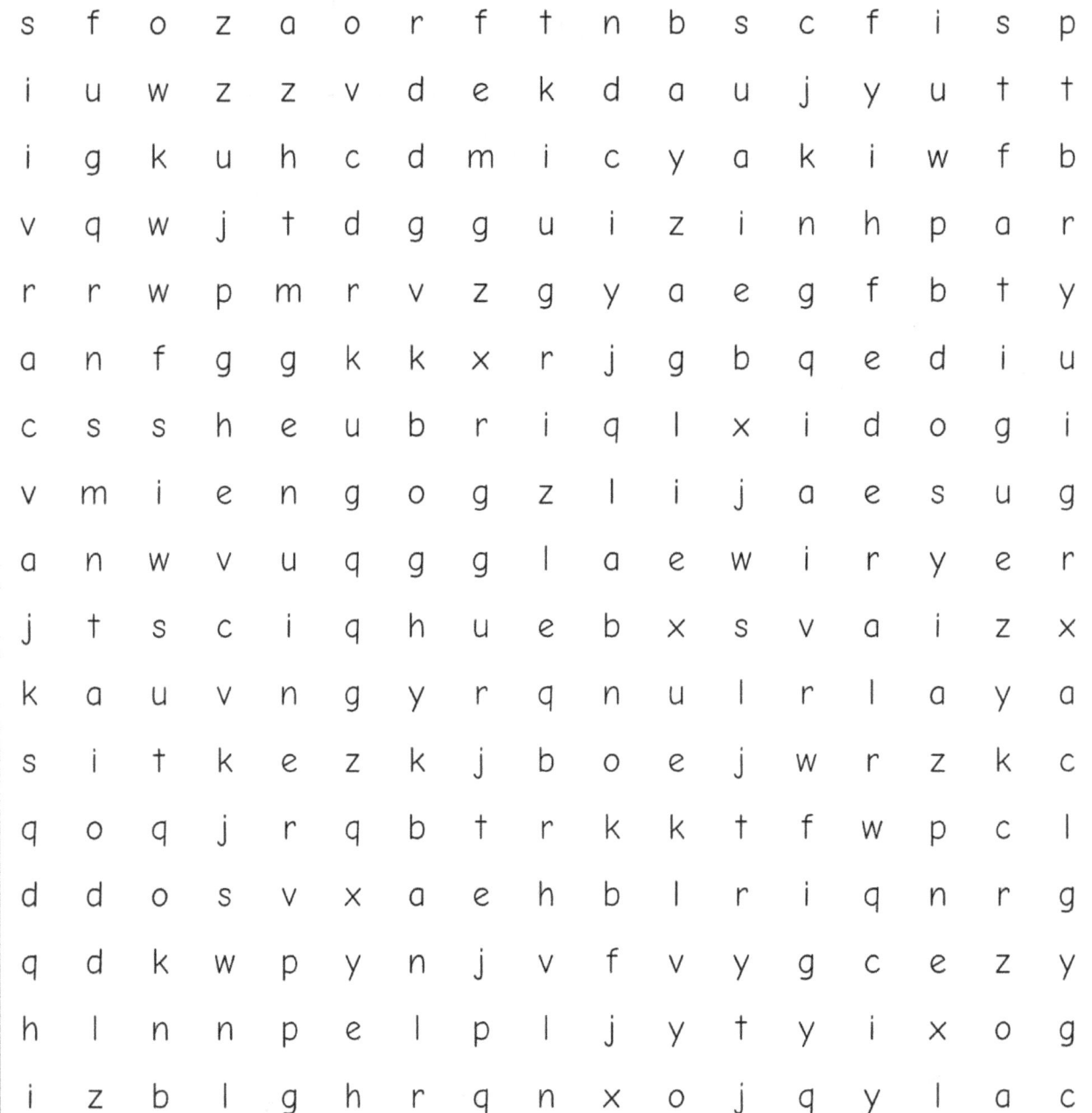

FATIGUE
FEDERAL
GENETIC
GENUINE

GENEROUS
GENIUS

What rhymes with these words

Fatigue   _____

Federal   _____

Generous   _____

Genetic   _____

Genius   _____

Genuine   _____

Find hidden words

Fatigue   _____

Federal   _____

Generous   _____

Genetic   _____

Genius   _____

Genuine   _____

Lesson 6

Re-write Words

Harsh			
Hazards			
Hispanic			
Historian			
Illusion			
Illustrate			

Find Letters

Harsh	m g h p d c a i g j s p r k a t p i s c a m d h e n
Hazards	g r o j h c d a q u i b z c a n p t r i l b a y e d s
Hispanic	z h e d b i k a n s c u p e a r g k n a g i w e c m
Historian	h k j i e l s i m o a k u t m o l g r i h y a d t n e
Illusion	a f d i u d g r l f q l n c u q s o f i j s o e t i n m
Illustrate	i p s f m l l x o u e s f t n r c i a u t c m o l e n c

These mnemonics are designed to create memorable associations or phrases that can help you remember the words better. Feel free to modify them or come up with your own mnemonics based on what helps you remember most effectively!

Harsh:
Mnemonic: "Howling Arctic Winds, Snow Heaps."

Hazards:
Mnemonic: "Hiking Across Zigzaggy, Rocky, Dangerous Slopes."

Hispanic:
Mnemonic: "Hot, Spicy, and Passionate Individuals Celebrate Ancestral Culture."

Historian:
Mnemonic: "Holding Intense Stories, Time Opens Records, Investigating Ancient Narratives."

Illusion:
Mnemonic: "Intriguing Lights Lure Unsuspecting Souls Into Otherworldly Nonsense."

Illustrate:
Mnemonic: "Imaginative Lines Lead Us Straight To Remarkable Artistic Exhibitions."

Find Meanings from Dictionary and write them here

Harsh _____

Hazards _____

Hispanic _____

Historian _____

Illusion _____

Illustrate _____

Write out these words in Capital letters

harsh _____

hazards _____

hispanic _____

historian _____

illusion _____

illustrate _____

Across

1. Relating to people of Spanish-speaking origin or descent.
3. To provide visual representation or examples.
5. Unpleasant or severe in nature.
6. A person who studies and writes about the past.

Down

2. A deceptive or misleading perception or belief.
4. Potential dangers or risks.

Write out the Synonyms and Antonyms of these words

	Synonyms	Antonyms
Harsh		
Hazards		
Hispanic		
Historian		
Illusion		
Illustrate		

Match the Unscramble Words

Harsh	sdharaz	....
Hazards	tornsihai	....
Hispanic	liuslno	....
Historian	tlutrelais	....
Illusion	rhahs	....
Illustrate	hcaisinp	....

"Complete the passage by using the words harsh, hazards, Hispanic, historian, illusion, and illustrate from this lesson."

"Throughout history, many _____ have studied and analyzed various aspects of different cultures and societies. One such scholar is the renowned _____ who delves deep into the past to understand and _____ the events and people of bygone eras. It is important to acknowledge that history can sometimes create _____ images or misinterpretations, leading to an _____ of reality. However, through careful research and examination, these historians strive to _____ the truth and provide accurate accounts of our collective past. They uncover the _____ and challenges faced by different communities, shedding light on the struggles and triumphs that have shaped our world."

Match the words to the shape

Harsh, Hazards, Hispanic, Historian, Illusion, Illustrate

Wordsearch

Puzzle# 6

```
I Y O S B L P F Y N L Y C I L Z
P A H F Y U J H R X F J O Z C S
N M Z L N E S Z J W A N L C F U
B I O B D R L W O S A Q T Q O Z
O L L P A V N N A I D C N I B X
B L L H D S U L R C J N H L F L
H U R G E V D O L C Y R Z L D K
N S I J Q E T N I G Z O S U K T
X I K G S S Q N Y H P V O S S N
U O O A I H A L O A A W C T F L
U N B H Q P O Z H Z Z O C R K Q
W D V F S F G U R A U C O A C P
D B X I Z P P T T R A T T T R L
N S H R U M F Q U D C X C E Y K
A D L D E B Y M Y S M A I U E V
H B E I O U I V D B N F S Y D N
```

HARSH   HAZARDS
HISPANIC   HISTORIAN
ILLUSION   ILLUSTRATE

What rhymes with these words

Harsh _____

Hazards _____

Hispanic _____

Historian _____

Illusion _____

Illustrate _____

Find hidden words

Harsh _____

Hazards _____

Hispanic _____

Historian _____

Illusion _____

Illustrate _____

Lesson 7

Re-write Words

Initial			
Initiate			
Inmate			
Innocence			
Join			
Joint			

Find Letters

Initial	I m g n p d m i g j s t p k a t p i u c a m d l
Initiate	g i o j n c d i q u t b i s c r a p t o l b a y e d
Inmate	z w i d b x k a n g c u m e a r g t a g l w e c
Innocence	l k j i e l n i m n a k o p m c e l g o n h y c e
Join	a f d j u d g r l f q t o c u q i o f r n j s e t i m
Joint	b p s f m k j x o u i f t n d c i a u c m o l t i n

These mnemonics are designed to create memorable associations or phrases that can help you remember the words better. Feel free to modify them or come up with your own mnemonics based on what helps you remember most effectively!

Initial:
Mnemonic: "I Never Imitate, That's Intentionally Always Learned."

Initiate:
Mnemonic: "I Now Introduce The Interesting And Terrific Idea, Telling Everyone."

Inmate:
Mnemonic: "I'm Not Inclined To Argue Much, Every time."

Innocence:
Mnemonic: "Innocent Newcomer, No Offense, Calmly Enjoying New Celebrations Entirely."

Join:
Mnemonic: "Jump Over, It's Now."

Joint:
Mnemonic: "Jack Ordered Ice Cream, No Toppings."

Find Meanings from Dictionary and write them here

Initial _____

Initiate _____

Inmate _____

Innocence _____

Join _____

Joint _____

Write out these words in Capital letters

initial _____

initiate _____

inmate _____

innocence _____

join _____

joint _____

Write out the Synonyms and Antonyms of these words

	Synonyms	Antonyms
Initial		
Initiate		
Inmate		
Innocence		
Join		
Joint		

Match the Unscramble Words

Initial	cocineenn	....
Initiate	tionj	....
Inmate	tlaniii	....
Innocence	nijo	....
Join	ntteiiia	....
Joint	niamet	....

Across

1. First or beginning.
4. Shared or done in cooperation with others.
5. The state of being innocent or free from guilt.

Down

2. A person confined to a prison or correctional facility.
3. To start or begin.
4. To come together or unite.

"Complete the Passage by filling in the blanks with the words you've learned in this lesson."

"When someone enters a new project or endeavor, it is important to have a clear _____ plan to set the course. The first step is to _____ the process by taking action and laying the foundation.
Similarly, when an individual becomes an _____ within the prison system, it is crucial to protect their _____ until proven guilty.
It is essential for everyone to _____ forces and work together towards a common goal. Through _____ efforts and collaboration, we can achieve greater success and positive outcomes."

Match the words to the shape

Initial, Initiate, Inmate, Innocence Join, Joint

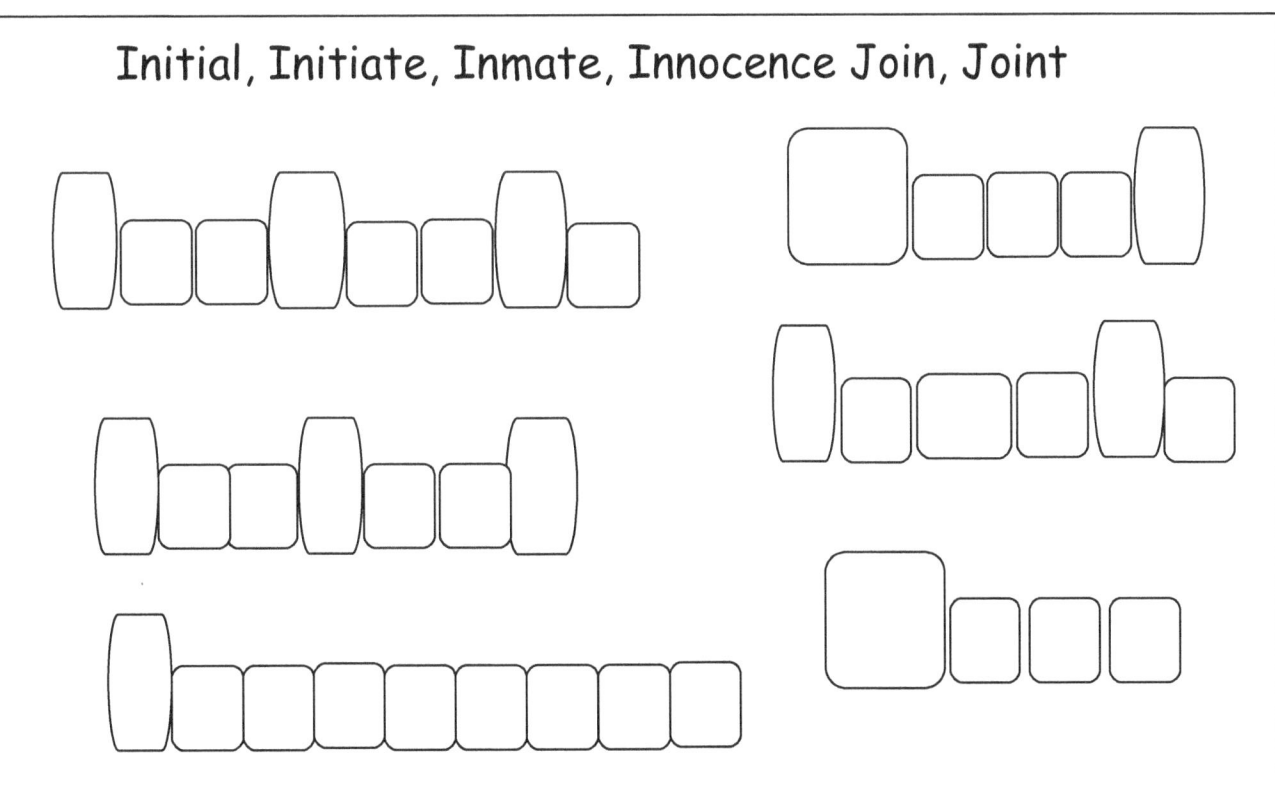

Wordsearch

Puzzle# 7

y	i	n	g	d	u	j	k	p	s	b	t	r	y	d	x
w	i	n	u	k	f	l	s	k	w	k	h	l	z	d	t
c	j	b	i	n	z	u	v	n	p	a	c	e	a	h	o
c	v	f	p	t	k	z	e	g	p	n	z	e	j	t	a
k	t	r	x	g	i	t	z	l	a	u	c	f	i	r	t
l	d	k	n	m	a	a	x	y	i	g	d	t	e	s	l
k	m	d	v	m	a	v	t	s	n	d	n	l	t	q	o
p	h	k	n	h	l	v	d	e	s	i	g	d	v	e	s
i	i	i	g	v	p	g	l	w	o	j	u	m	c	l	i
y	b	q	c	l	j	e	o	j	m	l	x	n	a	e	u
f	s	p	w	x	n	n	q	q	h	k	e	i	e	y	z
n	i	f	t	z	i	k	p	b	h	c	t	w	l	q	u
e	k	n	e	o	d	l	p	q	o	i	q	o	e	o	i
p	h	c	j	v	m	k	h	n	n	y	e	y	l	j	w
w	s	l	l	l	p	n	n	i	v	b	v	j	x	n	y
g	h	b	l	g	c	i	h	g	j	v	o	c	a	s	i

initial   initiate
inmate   innocence
join   joint

What rhymes with these words

Initial　　　_____

Initiate　　_____

Inmate　　　_____

Innocence　_____

Join　　　　_____

Joint　　　　_____

Find hidden words

Initial　　　_____

Initiate　　_____

Inmate　　　_____

Innocence　_____

Join　　　　_____

Joint　　　　_____

Lesson 8

Re-write Words

Insect			
Inspect			
Jewel			
Jury			
Knife			
Knock			

Find Letters

Jewel	M g o p s m d h r g j r t a p e k l w p e z x p l o i
Jury	g r o j n b m q u b p v r s r k l g y j a v n r u t r n
Insect	z w p i k a n h d s r y e c b v m k d a j t h d g n
Inspect	L k j i a l n d w r s l k g p q w b d e x y c h g l o t
Knife	A b d k c d g o p a s n g h r i q x e f h r c j k e t
Knock	B p s r c k l q p n d f j o d l s h a d c t f d l k p w

These mnemonics are designed to create memorable associations or phrases that can help you remember the words better. Feel free to modify them or come up with your own mnemonics based on what helps you remember most effectively!

Jewel:
Mnemonic: "Jolly Elves Wear Elegant Luxurious jewelry."

Jury:
Mnemonic: "Judges Usually Render a Verdict, You know?"

Insect:
Mnemonic: "Inquisitive Noses Seek Exotic Creepy Things."

Inspect:
Mnemonic: "Inspectors Now Systematically Probe Every Corner Tactfully."

Knife:
Mnemonic: "Keep Nice, It's For Eating."

Knock:
Mnemonic: "Kind Neighbors Offer Cheerful Knocks."

Find Meanings from Dictionary and write them here

Insect _____

Inspect _____

Jewel _____

Jury _____

Knife _____

Knock _____

Write out these words in Capital letters

insect _____

inspect _____

jewel _____

jury _____

knife _____

knock _____

Write out the Synonyms and Antonyms of these words

	Synonyms	Antonyms
Insect		
Inspect		
Jewel		
Jury		
Knife		
Knock		

Match the Unscramble Words

Insect	lewje	....
Inspect	feikn	....
Jewel	cokkn	....
Jury	ptsncie	....
Knife	snicet	....
Knock	rjuy	....

Complete the passage by filling in the blanks with the words you've learned in this lesson.

"As I walked through the forest, I came across a colorful _____ resting on a flower petal. Intrigued by its beauty, I decided to _____ it closer. Just as I bent down, I heard a soft _____ behind me. I turned around to find a hiker asking for directions. Startled, I accidentally dropped my _____ on the ground. Thankfully, it landed safely without causing any harm. After helping the hiker, I continued my exploration, keeping the image of that dazzling _____ in my mind."

Match the words to the shape

Jewel   Jury   Insect   Inspect   Knife   Knock

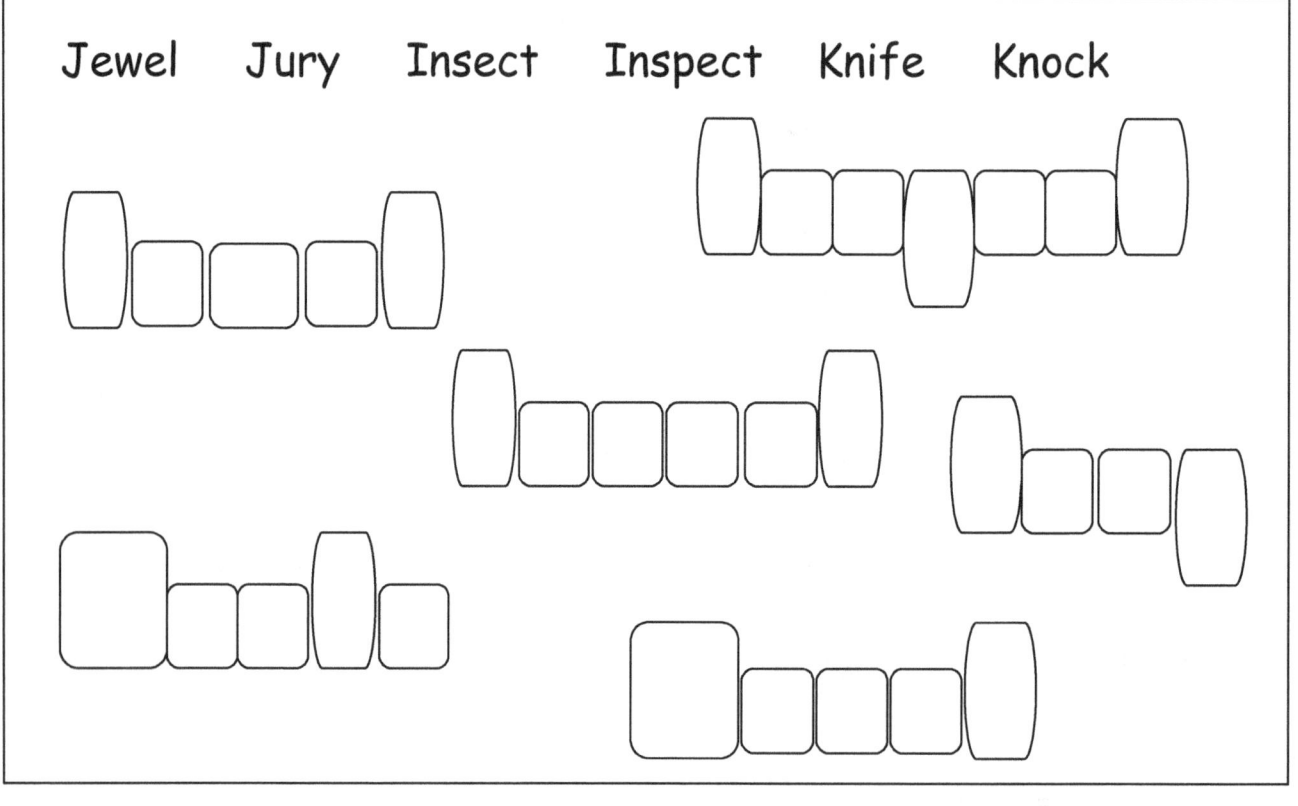

Wordsearch

Lesson # 8

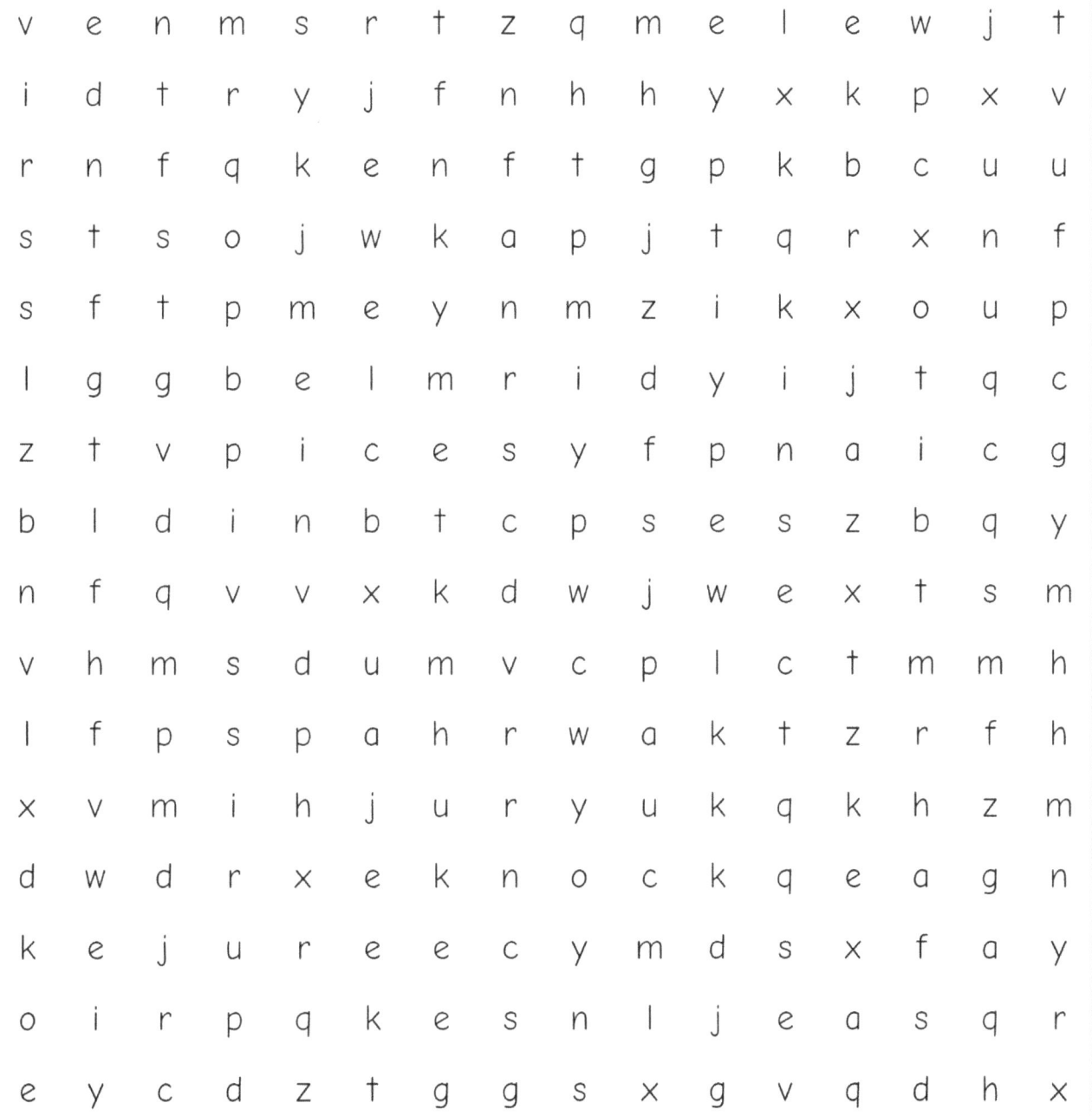

insect inspect
jewel jury
knife knock

What rhymes with these words

Insect _____

Inspect _____

Jewel _____

Jury _____

Knife _____

Knock _____

Find hidden words

Insect _____

Inspect _____

Jewel _____

Jury _____

Knife _____

Knock _____

Across

4. A small creature with six legs and typically has an exoskeleton.

5. A precious or valuable gem or stone.

Down

1. A sound made by striking or tapping on a surface.

2. A tool or instrument used for cutting or slicing.

3. To closely examine or investigate something.

5. A group of people selected to make a decision in a legal case.

Lesson 9

Re-write Words

Junior			
Juror			
Known			
Knowledge			
Landmark			
Landscape			

Find Letters

Junior	m g j p d c m i g u s p n k a t p i u c o m r h e
Juror	g r o j n c d o q u i b s c r n p t o i l b a y r d
Known	z w e d b x k a n g c o h e a w g k n a g l w e
Knowledge	l k j i e l n i m o a w u l m e d g o r e h y e d t
Landmark	a f d l u d g a l f q t n c d q i o m a n j r e k i m
Landscape	b p s l m k a x o n e f t n d s i a c a c m o p i e

These mnemonics are designed to create memorable associations or phrases that can help you remember the words better. Feel free to modify them or come up with your own mnemonics based on what helps you remember most effectively!

Junior:
Mnemonic: "Just Understand, Newcomers In Our Ranks."

Juror:
Mnemonic: "Judicial Understanding, Reviewing Our Responsibility."

Known:
Mnemonic: "Keep Observing, We Now Have Noted."

Knowledge:
Mnemonic: "Keep Nurturing Our Wisdom, Learn, and Get Educated."

Landmark:
Mnemonic: "Landmarks Are Notable Distinctive Markers, Always Recognizable."

Landscape:
Mnemonic: "Look Around, Notice Different Scenes, Captivating, and Peaceful."

Find Meanings from Dictionary and write them here

Junior _____

Juror _____

Known _____

Knowledge _____

Landmark _____

Landscape _____

Write out these words in Capital letters

Junior _____

Juror _____

Known _____

Knowledge _____

Landmark _____

Landscape _____

Write out the Synonyms and Antonyms of these words

	Synonyms	Antonyms
Junior		
Juror		
Known		
Knowledge		
Landmark		
Landscape		

Match the Unscramble Words

Junior	pelcsdaan	....
Juror	legowekdn	....
Known	namrlkda	....
Knowledge	noruji	....
Landmark	orujr	....
Landscape	wnonk	....

Complete the passage by filling in the blanks with the words you've learned in this lesson.

"As a _____ architect, I embarked on a journey to explore famous _____ and iconic _____ around the world. My thirst for _____ grew with every new _____ I encountered. One such breathtaking _____ was the Golden Gate Bridge in San Francisco. It is widely _____ for its magnificent design and engineering marvel. As I stood there, I felt a sense of pride being a _____ witness to such a remarkable structure that has become a part of the city's rich _____."

Match the words to the shape

Junior, Juror, Known, Knowledge, Landmark, Landscape

Across

2. A person of lower rank or experience, typically in a professional field.

4. A prominent or notable landmark or monument.

5. Facts, information, and skills acquired through experience or education.

Down

1. A member of a jury, responsible for deciding the verdict in a trial.

3. Familiar or recognized by many people.

4. The visible features of an area of land, including its physical characteristics.

What rhymes with these words

Junior _____

Juror _____

Known _____

Knowledge _____

Landmark _____

Landscape _____

Find hidden words

Junior _____

Juror _____

Known _____

Knowledge _____

Landmark _____

Landscape _____

Wordsearch

Lesson # 9

f	f	c	h	c	h	d	a	l	k	h	k	l	v	n	c
r	b	d	i	j	a	i	h	z	d	p	k	g	a	r	z
e	j	w	p	u	z	e	y	l	k	k	n	v	o	y	b
m	p	s	m	n	n	d	o	z	p	e	o	k	f	p	t
f	j	j	z	i	h	v	i	z	p	i	w	c	v	c	s
n	e	r	d	o	f	m	t	a	a	m	l	f	d	x	a
h	s	m	b	r	z	b	c	z	g	k	e	u	x	p	g
m	p	h	j	n	n	s	m	z	r	b	d	u	u	r	r
y	c	p	b	q	d	l	r	a	f	x	g	p	o	b	y
p	a	q	c	n	s	p	m	s	e	b	e	r	g	j	n
w	s	b	a	b	q	d	e	z	k	w	u	c	h	m	u
j	a	l	a	m	n	z	s	j	x	j	e	o	w	q	h
g	m	g	j	a	d	k	n	o	w	n	c	k	b	m	k
a	g	q	l	n	u	m	n	e	k	t	w	u	f	o	g
q	c	v	e	q	x	t	g	m	c	t	z	e	q	n	n
u	w	t	k	a	e	l	o	i	i	r	h	z	b	c	q

junior   juror
knowledge   known
landmark   landscape

Lesson 10

Re-write Words

Later			
Litre			
Metre			
Mere			
Merit			
Meter			

Find Letters

Later	m g l p a c m i g j s p k a t p i e c a m d h r e c
Litre	g r o j n c l o q u i b s c r t p o i l b r a y e d m
Metre	z m e d b x k a n g c t u h e a r g k n a g l w e
Mere	l k j i e l n i m o a k u e p m l g o r e h y e d t p
Merit	m f d l e d g r l f q n c u q i o f r n j s e t i m o
Meter	b p s f m k l x o u e f t n d c i a e c m o l r i n g

These mnemonics are designed to create memorable associations or phrases that can help you remember the words better. Feel free to modify them or come up with your own mnemonics based on what helps you remember most effectively!

Later:
Mnemonic: "Let's Arrange Time for Evening Relaxation."

Litre:
Mnemonic: "Liquid In The Red Erlenmeyer."

Metre:
Mnemonic: "Measure Every Tape, Repeatedly and Exactly."

Mere:
Mnemonic: "My Elder Relative's Experience."

Merit:
Mnemonic: "My Efforts Rewarded, I Triumphed."

Meter:
Mnemonic: "Measure Every Tiny Element's Reading."

Find Meanings from Dictionary and write them here

Later _____

Litre _____

Metre _____

Mere _____

Merit _____

Meter _____

Write out these words in Capital letters

later _____

litre _____

metre _____

mere _____

merit _____

meter _____

Write out the Synonyms and Antonyms of these words

	Synonyms	Antonyms
Later		
Litre		
Metre		
Mere		
Merit		
Meter		

Match the Unscramble Words

Later	tmeer	....
Litre	tirme	....
Metre	mree	....
Mere	emtre	....
Merit	tleri	....
Meter	tarle	....

Fill the blanks and underline the words you have learned in this lesson

1. Sarah poured 500 milliliters of water into the cylinder, which was equivalent to half a _____.

2. Sarah was fascinated by the concept of_____ measurements, where the metre is the basic unit of length and the litre is the unit of volume.

3. She recorded the measurement, noting the reading on the _____ scale of the cylinder.

4. Later, she conducted her experiment, analyzing the data and drawing conclusions based on the observed results.

5. Sarah's attention to detail and accuracy earned her high praise from her teacher, who commended her on the _____ of her work.

Match the words to the shape

Later, Litre, Metre, Mere, Merit, Meter

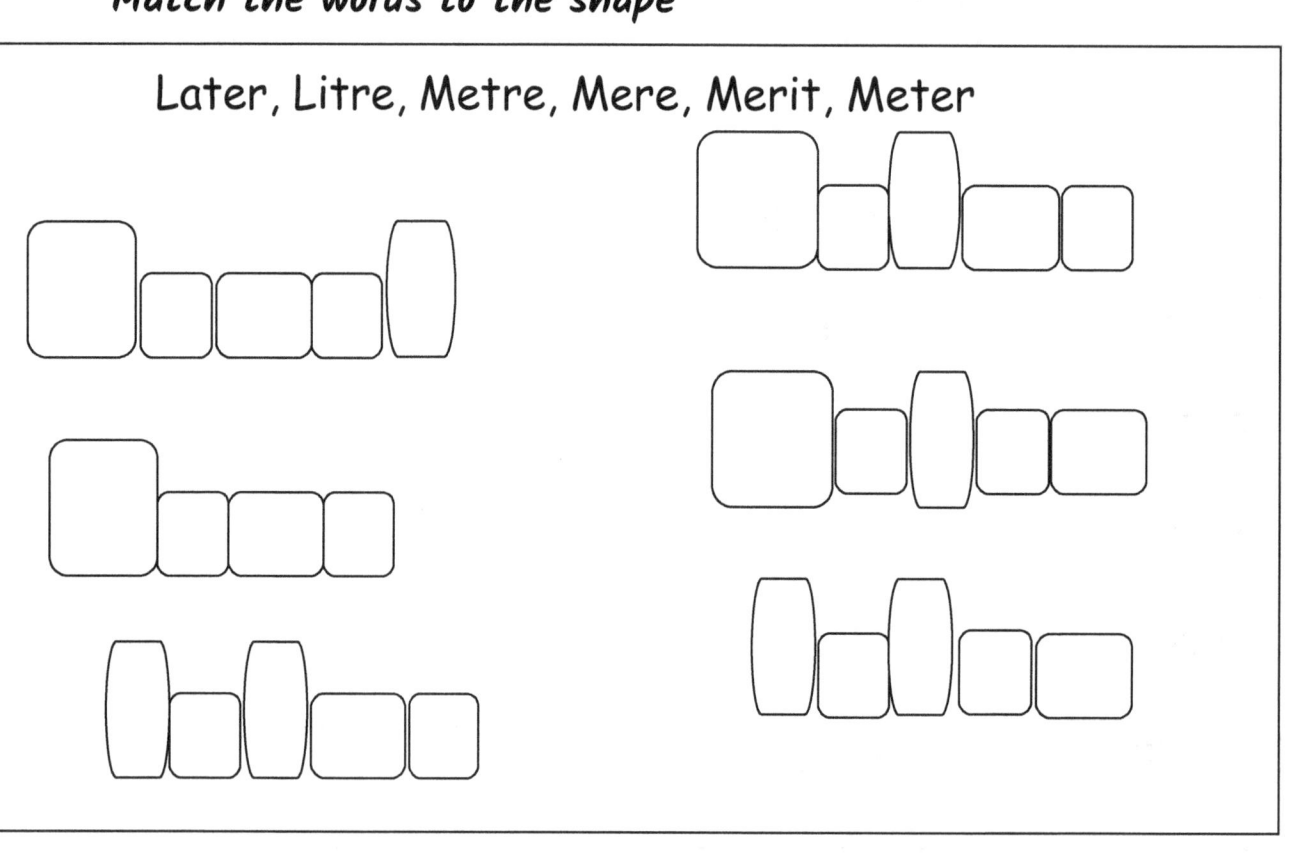

Reading Comprehension Passage

"Sarah was preparing for her science experiment. She carefully measured out the ingredients, using a graduated cylinder to ensure precise amounts. She poured 500 milliliters of water into the cylinder, which was equivalent to half a litre. Sarah was fascinated by the concept of metric measurements, where the metre is the basic unit of length and the litre is the unit of volume. She recorded the measurement, noting the reading on the metre scale of the cylinder. Later, she conducted her experiment, analyzing the data and drawing conclusions based on the observed results. Sarah's attention to detail and accuracy earned her high praise from her teacher, who commended her on the merit of her work."

Reading Comprehension Questions:

1. What did Sarah use to measure the ingredients for her experiment?

2. How many milliliters of water did Sarah pour into the cylinder?

3. Which unit of measurement is used for length in the metric system?

4. Which unit of measurement is used for volume in the metric system?

5. What earned Sarah high praise from her teacher?

Wordsearch

Lesson # 10

y	j	q	v	v	m	p	o	k	f	s	k	o	p	t	g
m	i	e	s	t	s	g	x	k	n	x	e	j	s	j	f
q	m	x	g	d	x	h	e	n	s	q	p	o	e	q	j
w	h	r	d	g	d	q	s	f	y	x	r	a	z	m	c
b	d	z	p	k	i	r	v	t	j	v	h	u	m	v	t
f	k	a	e	m	e	t	e	r	z	o	h	x	o	f	r
f	n	g	m	e	r	e	l	w	i	z	o	s	b	o	x
g	l	w	u	b	d	v	b	a	o	m	a	t	i	j	m
t	m	o	v	r	n	l	w	f	n	x	e	x	m	g	e
t	w	v	u	o	v	o	s	x	d	g	s	r	m	c	t
k	d	l	u	z	j	l	u	y	q	f	l	c	i	k	r
s	b	a	v	s	f	j	i	t	s	w	o	e	a	t	e
r	f	t	h	x	t	y	d	r	g	f	k	t	k	q	a
t	l	e	j	m	v	o	w	d	l	i	t	r	e	e	j
g	c	r	f	c	m	z	m	x	o	h	c	s	x	p	a
f	d	v	f	e	e	r	k	q	e	m	o	b	g	x	w

later   litre
mere   merit
meter   metre

Across
3. It is the basic unit of length in the metric system.
4. It is commonly used to measure liquids.

Down
1. A small and simple quantity or amount.
2. The worth or value of something based on qualities or achievements.
3. It typically has numerical markings or a scale to indicate measurements.
4. Synonym for "afterwards" or "at a subsequent time."

What rhymes with these words

Later _____

Litre _____

Metre _____

Mere _____

Merit _____

Meter _____

Find hidden words

Later _____

Litre _____

Metre _____

Mere _____

Merit _____

Meter _____

Lesson 11

Re-write Words

Measure			
Motion			
Nation			
Notion			
Network			
Networth			

Find Letters

Measure	M g o p e n a d h r g j s a p u k t w p r z x e p l
Motion	g r o m n b o q u e b p v t s r i l g o j a r u k r n
Nation	z w m p i e k n h d a r t e i b r o k d a j t n e p c
Notion	l k j i a n d m r s l k g o q w t d i x y o h g l n t p
Network	A b d l n d g i e l p t s n w h r o q x r f h r c j k t
Networth	B p n r m k e q p n t f j w d o s h d r t f d l h p w

These mnemonics are designed to create memorable associations or phrases that can help you remember the words better. Feel free to modify them or come up with your own mnemonics based on what helps you remember most effectively!

Measure:
Mnemonic: "Mark Every Single Segment, Understand and Record."

Motion:
Mnemonic: "Moving Objects Travel In One Direction."

Nation:
Mnemonic: "Nations Are Territories In One Network."

Notion:
Mnemonic: "New Opinions Take Interesting Outlooks, Noticing."

Network:
Mnemonic: "Numerous Entities Work Together, Operating Responsively, Keeping communication."

Networth:
Mnemonic: "Nurture Every Talent, Work Onwards, Reaping The Harvest."

Find Meanings from Dictionary and write them here

Measure _____

Motion _____

Nation _____

Notion _____

Network _____

Networth _____

Write out these words in Capital letters

measure _____

motion _____

nation _____

notion _____

network _____

networth _____

Write out the Synonyms and Antonyms of these words

	Synonyms	Antonyms
Measure		
Motion		
Nation		
Notion		
Network		
Networth		

Match the Unscramble Words

Measure	tnoina	....
Motion	tniono	....
Nation	ntmioo	....
Notion	worketn	....
Network	norhttew	....
Networth	maueres	....

Underline synonyms and antonyms of - Measure, Motion, Nation, Notion, Network, Networth

Assess, quantify, gauge, evaluate, Movement, action, activity, gesture, Country, state, homeland, territory, Idea, concept, belief, thought, Web, system, grid, interconnectedness, Wealth, assets, value, financial worth.

Guess, estimate, approximate, conjecture, Stillness, immobility, inaction, rest, Individual, person, citizen, resident., Fact, reality, certainty, truth, Disconnection, isolation, detachment, separation, liability, poverty, insolvency.

Match the words to the shape

Measure, Motion, Nation, Notion, Network, Networth

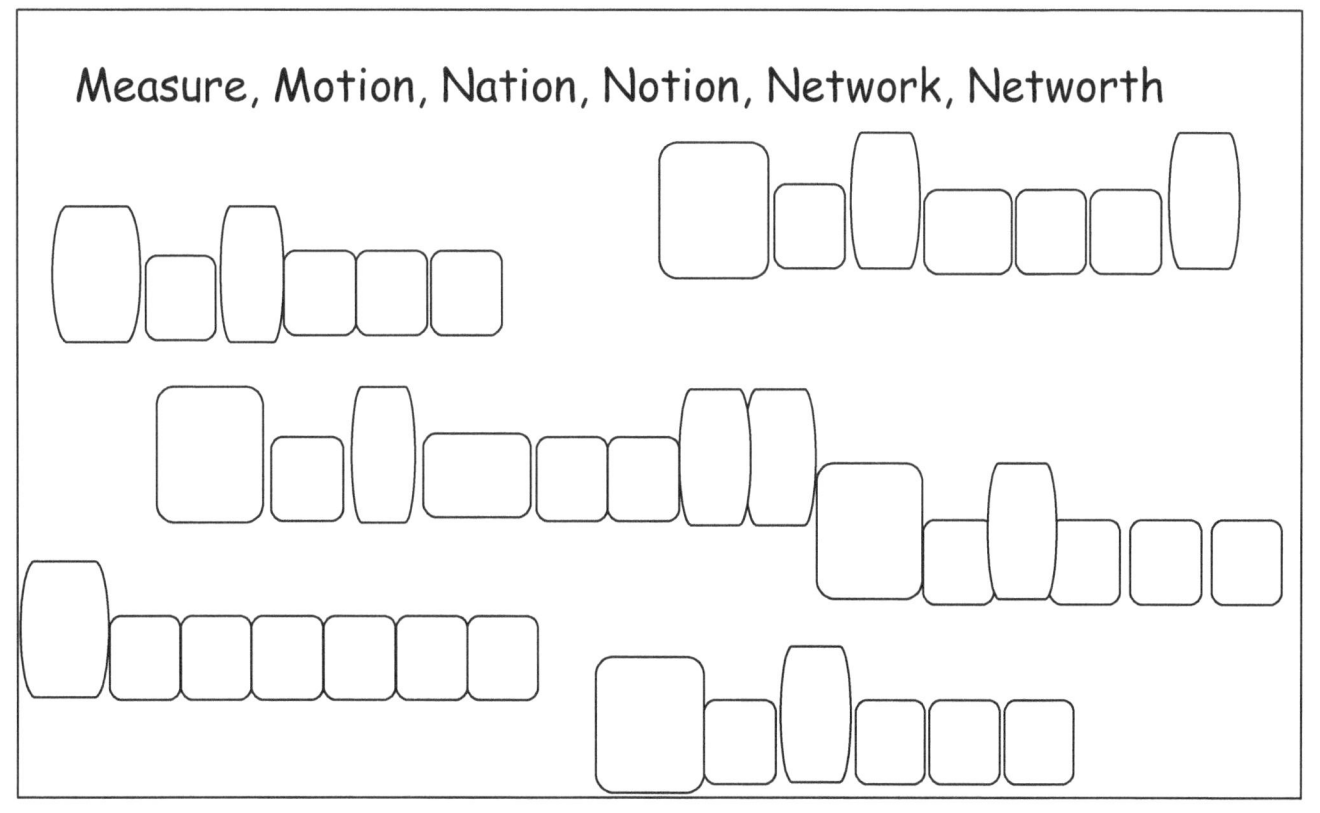

Across
1. Refers to movement, typically from one location to another.
3. A financial measure that calculates an individual's or company's wealth or value.
4. Refers to a series of interconnected nodes or individuals, facilitating communication or information exchange.

Down
1. To quantify or evaluate the size, length, or amount of something.
2. An idea or understanding about something, often subjective in nature.
3. A group of individuals sharing a common identity and typically residing within specific borders.

Reading Comprehension Passage

"Understanding the concept of time and motion is crucial in physics. Scientists use various instruments to _____ the distance traveled or speed of an object. These instruments provide precise _____ of the object's movement. Similarly, in the digital age, we are connected by a vast _____ of information known as the internet. This worldwide _____ allows us to communicate, share knowledge, and stay connected. Just as each individual is a part of a _____ community, every country is a member of the global _____. Each nation has its own unique characteristics and contributes to the global tapestry with its culture, ideas, and values. Success in the business world often involves the _____ of an individual or company. It is a measure of their financial value, assets, and investments."

Reading Comprehension Questions:

What do scientists use to determine the distance traveled or speed of an object?

What provides precise information about an object's movement?

What is the vast network of information known as in the digital age?

How does the internet enable communication and connection?

What does each country contribute to the global community?

Wordsearch

Lesson # 11

l	m	c	o	c	v	t	y	i	i	y	k	j	j
y	y	m	o	q	u	l	c	r	c	v	m	z	g	o
e	l	a	q	m	b	o	z	a	a	f	v	n	r	c
l	a	g	a	c	z	h	g	l	d	w	v	e	i	p	b
l	w	m	x	m	l	s	f	z	q	p	w	t	k	c	t
t	u	b	b	m	w	e	m	m	f	e	t	w	z	e	a
a	f	e	f	f	o	h	x	g	h	z	j	o	z	c	n
h	t	m	n	e	t	w	o	r	t	h	r	r	x	b	o
l	r	g	t	m	a	e	e	m	l	n	a	k	t	p	t
s	u	p	o	h	v	r	a	l	o	r	t	u	m	x	i
a	l	m	e	e	u	i	v	i	v	t	k	u	z	y	o
z	c	u	h	s	r	r	t	l	c	f	i	j	e	j	n
k	r	h	a	b	e	a	q	m	v	v	o	o	m	c	r
t	a	e	l	c	n	m	g	b	t	d	t	d	n	p	t
v	m	p	l	z	m	c	t	s	y	j	z	f	z	c	b
v	m	o	g	e	h	g	x	k	l	d	f	z	i	e	k

measure motion
nation network
networth notion

What rhymes with these words

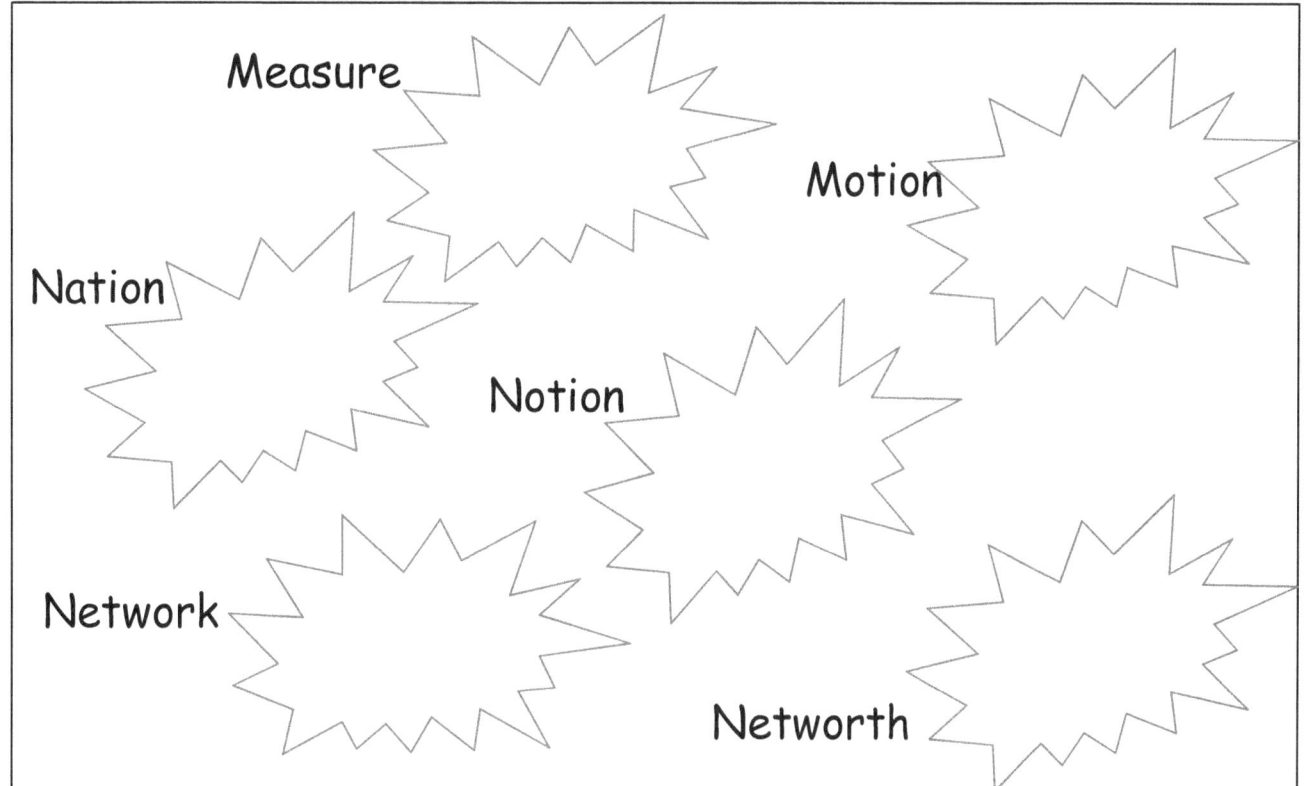

Measure
Motion
Nation
Notion
Network
Networth

Find hidden words

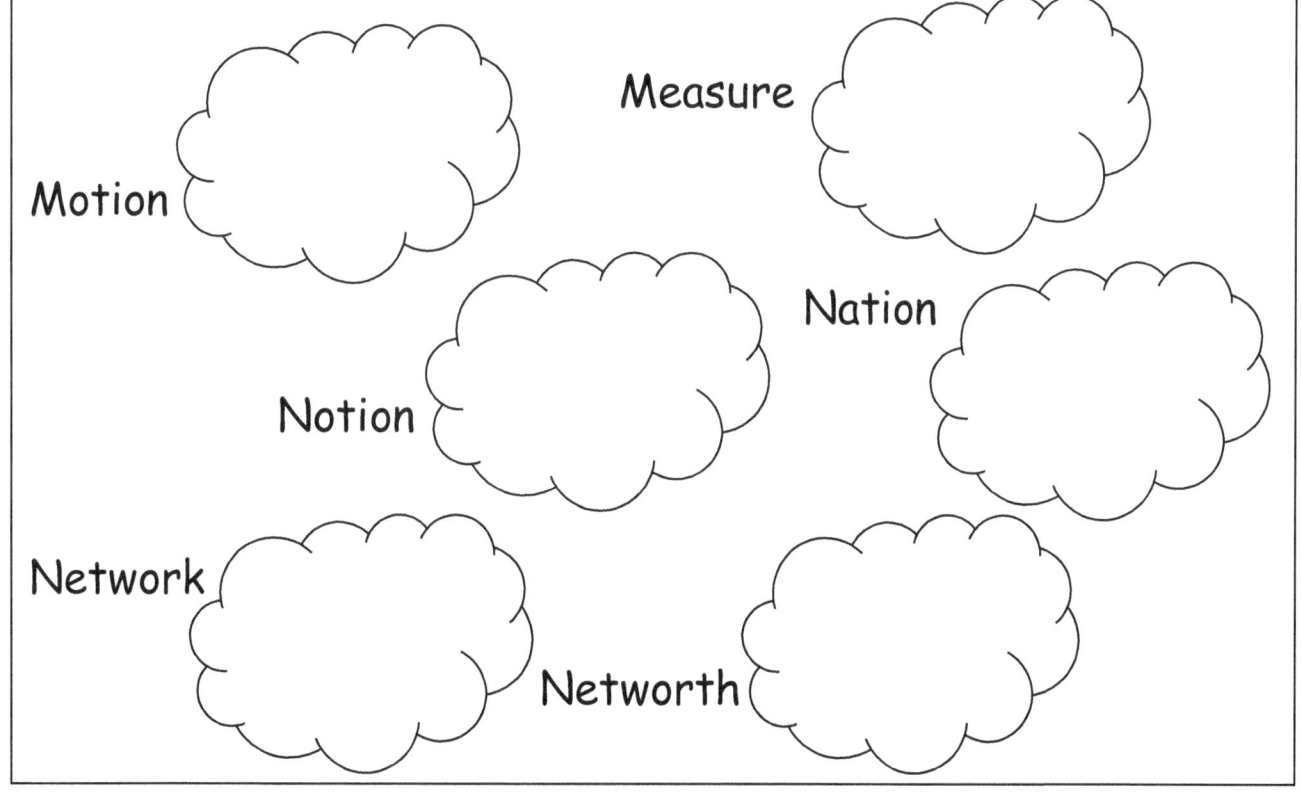

Motion
Measure
Notion
Nation
Network
Networth

Lesson 12

Re-write Words

Obvious			
Observe			
Opposition			
Optimistic			
Pale			
Palace			

Find Letters

Obvious	M g o p s n m b h r g j v a p i k t w p o z x u p s l
Observe	g r o j n b m q s e b p r v t s r w e g o j a r u k r
Opposition	z o m p i p k o n h d s r i u t c b i m o d a n t e p
Optimistic	L k j i o l p d t r i l k m o q i s t d i x y c h g l n t
Pale	A b d l c p g i o l a t s n g h r n l x e f h r c j k t
Palace	p s r m k l a p n e f l t d a h d r t f d l c e p w b

These mnemonics are designed to create memorable associations or phrases that can help you remember the words better. Feel free to modify them or come up with your own mnemonics based on what helps you remember most effectively!

Obvious:
Mnemonic: "Our Brains Easily Visualize Inherent Understanding, Simple."

Observe:
Mnemonic: "Open Both Eyes, Serve, and Visualize Every detail."

Opposition:
Mnemonic: "Other People's Positions Sit In Opposition, Supporting Individual Opinions Neatly."

Optimistic:
Mnemonic: "Overcome Problems, Trust In Successful Thinking, Inspire Confidence."

Pale:
Mnemonic: "Polar Bears Are Lightly Eclipsed."

Palace:
Mnemonic: "People Admire Lavish, Awe-inspiring Castles Every day."

Find Meanings from Dictionary and write them here

Obvious _____

Observe _____

Opposition _____

Optimistic _____

Pale _____

Palace _____

Write out these words in Capital letters

obvious _____

observe _____

opposition _____

optimistic _____

pale _____

palace _____

Write out the Synonyms and Antonyms of these words

	Synonyms	Antonyms
Obvious		
Observe		
Opposition		
Optimistic		
Pale		
Palace		

Match the Unscramble Words

Obvious	tnoina	....
Observe	tniono	....
Opposition	ntmioo	....
Optimistic	worketn	....
Pale	norhttew	....
Palace	maueres	....

Fill the blanks using the words you have learned in this lesson

"As I entered the grand _____ , the elegance and magnificence of the surroundings were _____. The intricate details and ornate decorations adorned the walls, giving the palace a regal atmosphere. I couldn't help but _____ the opulence and splendor that surrounded me. Amidst the grandeur, I noticed a group of people engaged in a lively debate, expressing their _____ to each other. Despite their differing views, they remained _____ and hopeful for a better future. The vibrant colors and lively discussions created a beautiful contrast against the _____ hues of the palace walls."

Match the words to the shape

Obvious, Observe, Opposition, Optimistic, Pale, Palace

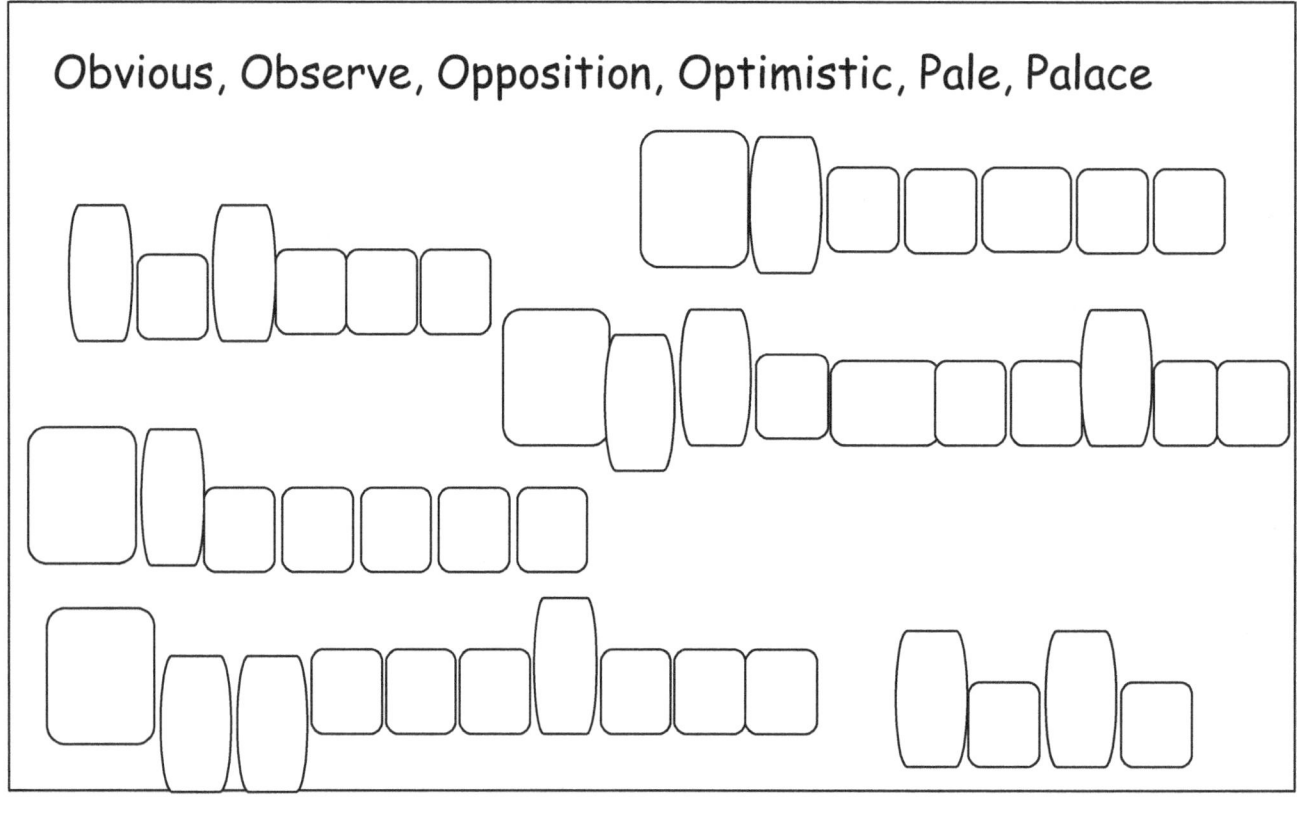

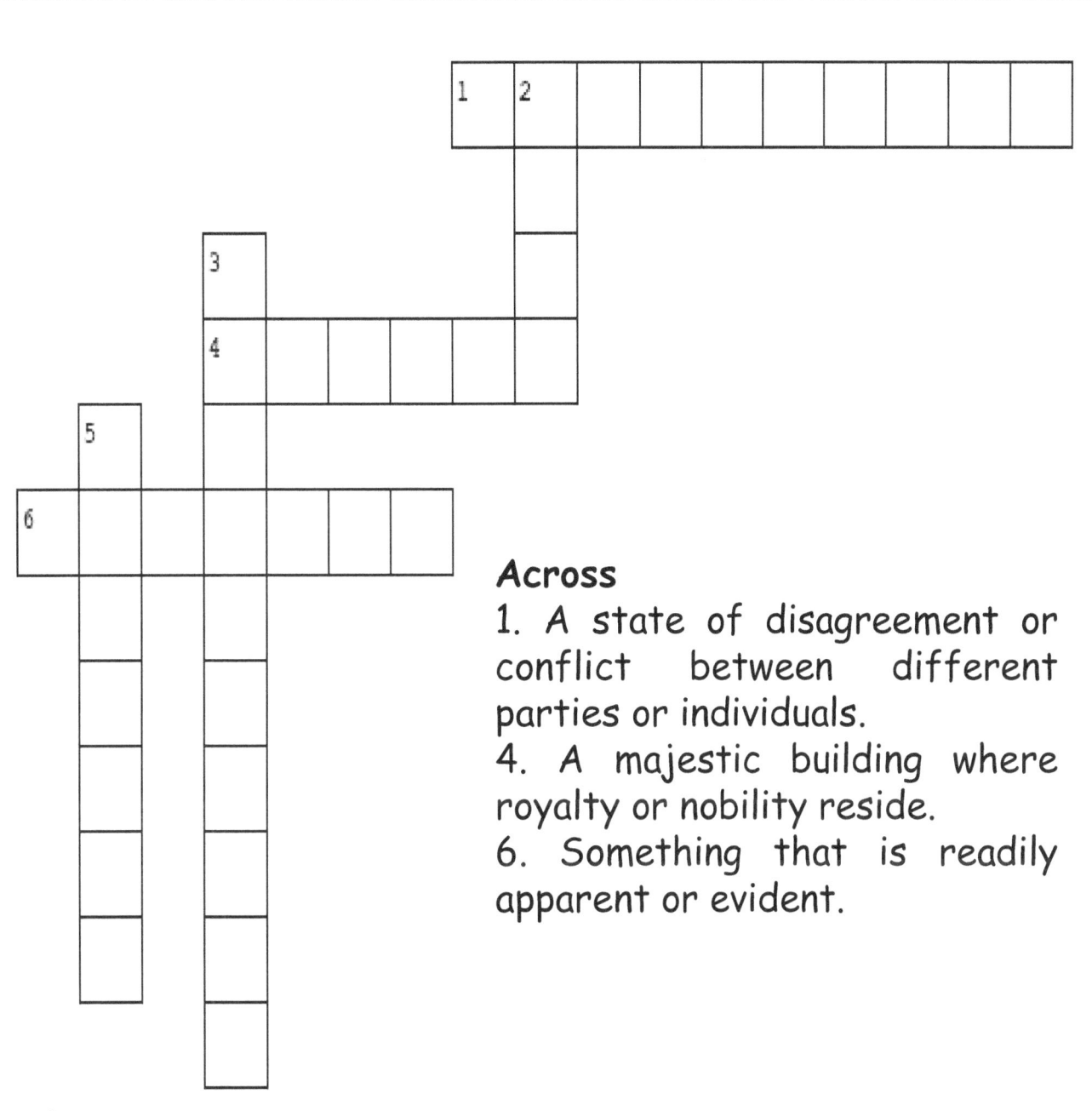

Across
1. A state of disagreement or conflict between different parties or individuals.
4. A majestic building where royalty or nobility reside.
6. Something that is readily apparent or evident.

Down
2. Referring to a light or washed-out color, often associated with a lack of vibrancy or saturation.
3. A mindset or attitude that expects positive outcomes or looks for the best in a situation.
5. To pay close attention to something, usually with the purpose of gaining information or understanding.

What rhymes with these words

Obvious

Observe

Opposition

Optimistic

Pale

Palace

Find hidden words

Obvious

Observe

Opposition

Optimistic

Palace

Pale

Wordsearch

Lesson # 12

E	S	Z	P	C	E	T	P	A	H	P	B	V	S	T
Y	O	R	U	S	F	B	F	O	A	U	Y	T	T	G	X
K	P	O	W	H	E	M	C	N	B	L	Y	Y	P	U	F
A	P	P	B	G	G	X	W	G	H	E	M	Y	A	U	C
Q	O	T	L	W	O	I	T	A	J	L	Y	X	W	I	W
H	S	I	T	E	B	M	P	K	B	O	X	H	J	F	Z
F	I	M	J	E	S	K	W	J	V	T	V	K	B	S	T
V	T	I	X	A	E	L	B	F	T	G	E	Z	M	Z	K
G	I	S	I	R	R	G	A	P	R	E	T	E	D	R	N
D	O	T	O	B	V	I	O	U	S	N	E	E	G	X	E
J	N	I	I	T	E	Z	H	Q	O	P	A	L	A	C	E
F	X	C	L	T	K	X	B	D	Z	O	U	U	C	I	F
N	V	O	S	Y	G	E	X	P	A	L	E	E	I	A	K
I	L	C	B	B	Z	D	E	D	R	I	Q	W	G	T	N
R	G	W	B	Q	G	V	J	Q	V	E	J	U	H	F	W
X	Y	Z	I	T	S	I	F	P	E	O	X	T	F	I	Z

OBSERVE   OBVIOUS?
OPPOSITION   OPTIMISTIC
PALACE   PALE

Lesson 13

Re-write Words

Peak			
Peek			
Peace			
Piece			
Quiet			
Quite			

Find Letters

Peak	M g o p s n e d h r g j r a p e k t w p i z x o p l n
Peek	g r o j n b m p u e b p v t s r w l g e j a r u k r n
Peace	z w m p i e k a n h d s r u c b r m k d a j t e p l
Piece	L k j i a p n d m i s l k g e q w t d i c y o h g e n
Quiet	A q d l c d g u o l p t s i g h r n q x e f t r c j k h
Quite	B p s q m k l p n u e f j t d i s h a d r t f d l e p w

Here are some mnemonic examples for the given words to facilitate comprehension:

1. Peak: "Peak" sounds like "peek." Imagine climbing to the top of a mountain to "peek" at the stunning view from the peak.

2. Peek: "Peek" sounds like "peak." Visualize someone taking a quick "peek" over a hill or from behind a corner to see what's there.

3. Peace: "Peace" rhymes with "ease." Picture yourself in a tranquil setting, where everything is calm and easygoing, promoting a sense of peace.

4. Piece: "Piece" sounds like "peace." Imagine putting together the pieces of a puzzle, which brings a sense of completion and peace.

5. Quiet: "Quiet" sounds like "quiet." Picture a library, where people are reading and studying in a serene and hushed environment.

6. Quite: "Quite" sounds like "quiet." Think of someone whispering softly, saying something in a gentle and subdued manner.

Find Meanings from Dictionary and write them here

Peak _____

Peek _____

Peace _____

Piece _____

Quiet _____

Quite _____

Write out these words in Capital letters

peak _____

peek _____

peace _____

piece _____

quiet _____

quite _____

Wordsearch

Lesson # 13

I	C	N	R	X	X	E	S	B	N	B	M	D	W	T
N	M	X	J	R	W	A	E	H	I	P	Z	R	D	N
Y	N	P	J	C	I	D	H	W	A	W	G	N	Q	Z
V	P	B	W	G	Q	J	E	F	P	B	X	X	P	S
K	V	E	C	L	U	A	T	U	E	L	P	T	Y	Z
W	Q	G	A	V	I	D	I	M	E	N	D	F	I	J
S	L	K	V	K	E	Z	N	S	K	S	Z	K	L	A
Y	S	I	S	W	T	H	C	W	O	U	N	H	P	U
M	D	S	H	Y	R	N	S	B	P	D	G	H	J	O
I	X	P	B	N	B	W	D	X	I	A	L	D	B	E
W	U	I	F	Y	K	Y	R	X	Z	T	E	N	T	K
Q	Q	E	Q	S	E	L	K	N	O	J	K	I	I	G
D	D	C	B	L	X	O	C	W	W	B	U	D	B	Q
Y	C	E	Z	Z	X	X	A	N	A	Q	X	E	Z	V
W	L	N	U	G	T	R	H	Z	W	U	F	N	B	U
E	L	K	M	D	C	T	A	K	Q	Q	P	R	E	K

PEACE   PEAK
PEEK   PIECE
QUIET   QUITE

Write out the Synonyms and Antonyms of these words

	Synonyms	Antonyms
Peak		
Peek		
Peace		
Piece		
Quiet		
Quite		

Match the Unscramble Words

Peak	ecpei	....
Peek	epeac	....
Peace	ekpe	....
Piece	kepa	....
Quiet	tqiue	....
Quite	tiqeu	....

Fill the blanks and Make the sentences using above words

"At the top of the mountain, I reached the highest _____, where I could see a breathtaking view. I took a quick _____ over the edge to admire the scenery below. The serene surroundings brought a sense of tranquility and _____. I felt a sense of completion as if I had found the missing _____. The atmosphere was calm and _____.
It was _____ the perfect moment to reflect and enjoy the peacefulness."

Match the words to the shape

Peak, Peek, Peace, Piece, Quiet, Quite

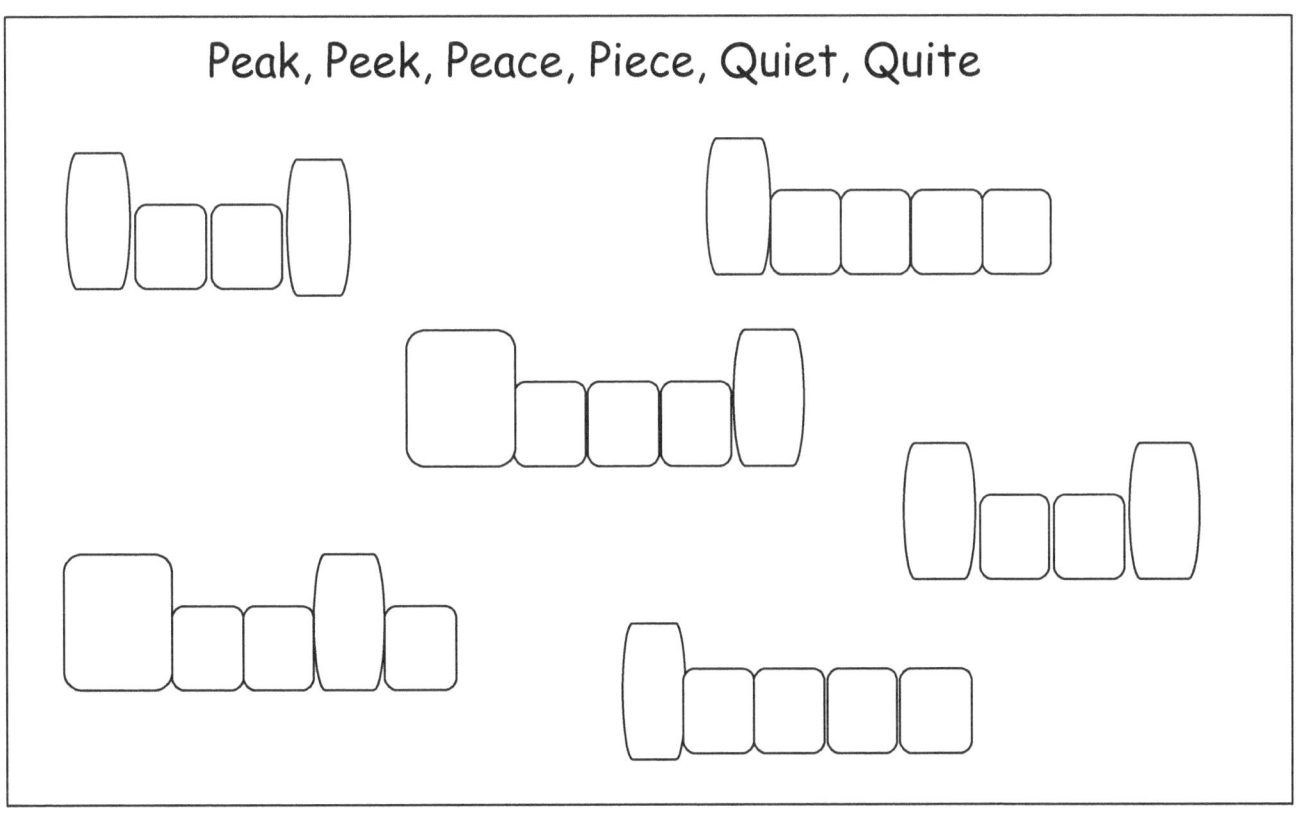

Across

4. A peaceful condition characterized by calmness, serenity, and freedom from disturbance.
5. The topmost part or apex of something, often associated with mountains.

Down

1. To a certain degree or extent, often used to emphasize or qualify a statement.
2. A fragment or component that is part of a larger entity or object.
3. A state of calm, stillness, or absence of sound or commotion.
4. To glance or sneak a brief look at something or someone.

Lesson 14

Re-write Words

Quit			
Quick			
Quote			
Quest			
Receive			
Release			

Find Letters

Quit	M g q p u n m d h i g j r a p e k t w p i z x o p l n
Quick	g r o q n b m q u e b p i t s r w l g c j a r u k r n
Quote	z q m p i u k a n h d s r o u e c b r t k d a j e p m
Quest	L k j i a q n d u r e l k g s q w t d i x y o h g l n t
Receive	A r d l e c d g o l p t e n g h i n q x v f h r e j k t
Release	B p s r m k l q p n e f j t l s h e d a t f s l e p w b

These mnemonics are designed to create memorable associations or phrases that can help you remember the words better. Feel free to modify them or come up with your own mnemonics based on what helps you remember most effectively!

Quit:
Mnemonic: "Quit Unproductive, Irritating Tasks."

Quick:
Mnemonic: "Quickly Understand, It's Convenient, Keep."

Quote:
Mnemonic: "Quoting Others' Ideas Takes Eloquence."

Quest:
Mnemonic: "Questing Unveils Exciting Secrets, Thrills."

Receive:
Mnemonic: "Receiving Every Card, I Value Each."

Release:
Mnemonic: "Relax, Enjoy, Let Everything And Stress Escape."

Match the Meanings with the following words

Quit — A journey or pursuit undertaken in search of something.

Quick — A memorable or noteworthy statement from a source.

Quote — To come into possession or acquire something.

Quest — To set free or let go.

Receive — Marked by high speed or swiftness.

Release — To leave or resign from a job or position.

Write out these words in Capital letters

quit _____

quick _____

quote _____

quest _____

receive _____

release _____

Fill the blanks of this passage with synonyms of words you have learned in this lesson - Pursuit, Obtain, Free, Depart, Rapid, Saying

"I decided to _____ my job and explore new opportunities. It was time for a change, and I wanted to embark on a _____ journey to find my true passion. During this adventure, I came across an inspiring _____ that motivated me to keep going. It fueled my determination and strengthened my _____ for self-discovery. Along the way, I encountered helpful mentors who were willing to _____ their wisdom and guidance. Their support gave me the confidence to _____ my fears and embrace new possibilities."

Match the Unscramble Words

Quit	equto	....
Quick	stequ	....
Quote	cqiuk	....
Quest	tiuq	....
Receive	sreeale	....
Release	veecrei	....

Across

2. To stop or give up one's employment or role.
4. An expedition or adventure with a specific goal or objective.
5. To be given or obtain something.

Down

1. A notable phrase or passage cited from someone or something.
3. To liberate or allow something or someone to be free.
4. Characterized by rapid or fast movement or action.

What rhymes with these words

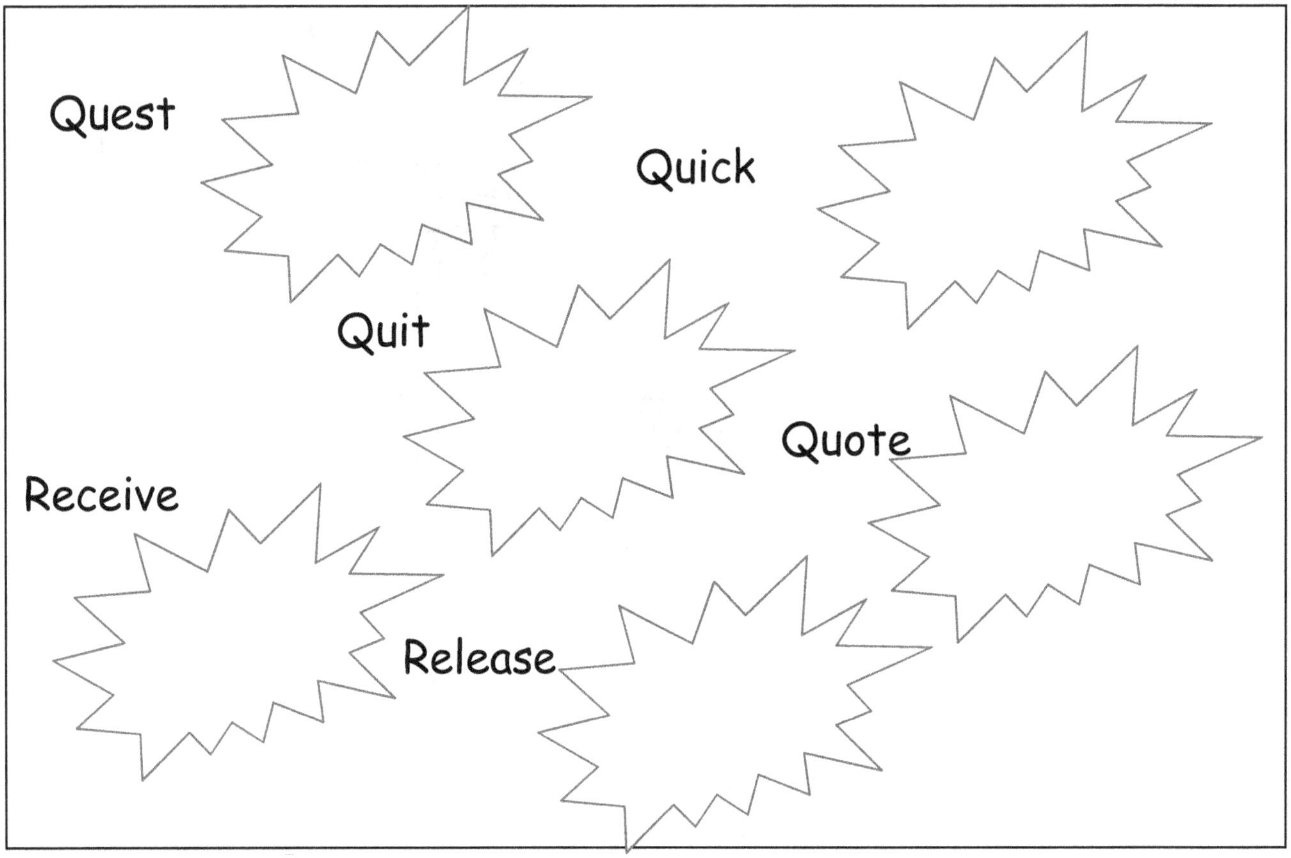

Quest

Quick

Quit

Quote

Receive

Release

Match the words to the shape

Quit, Quick, Quote, Quest, Receive, Release

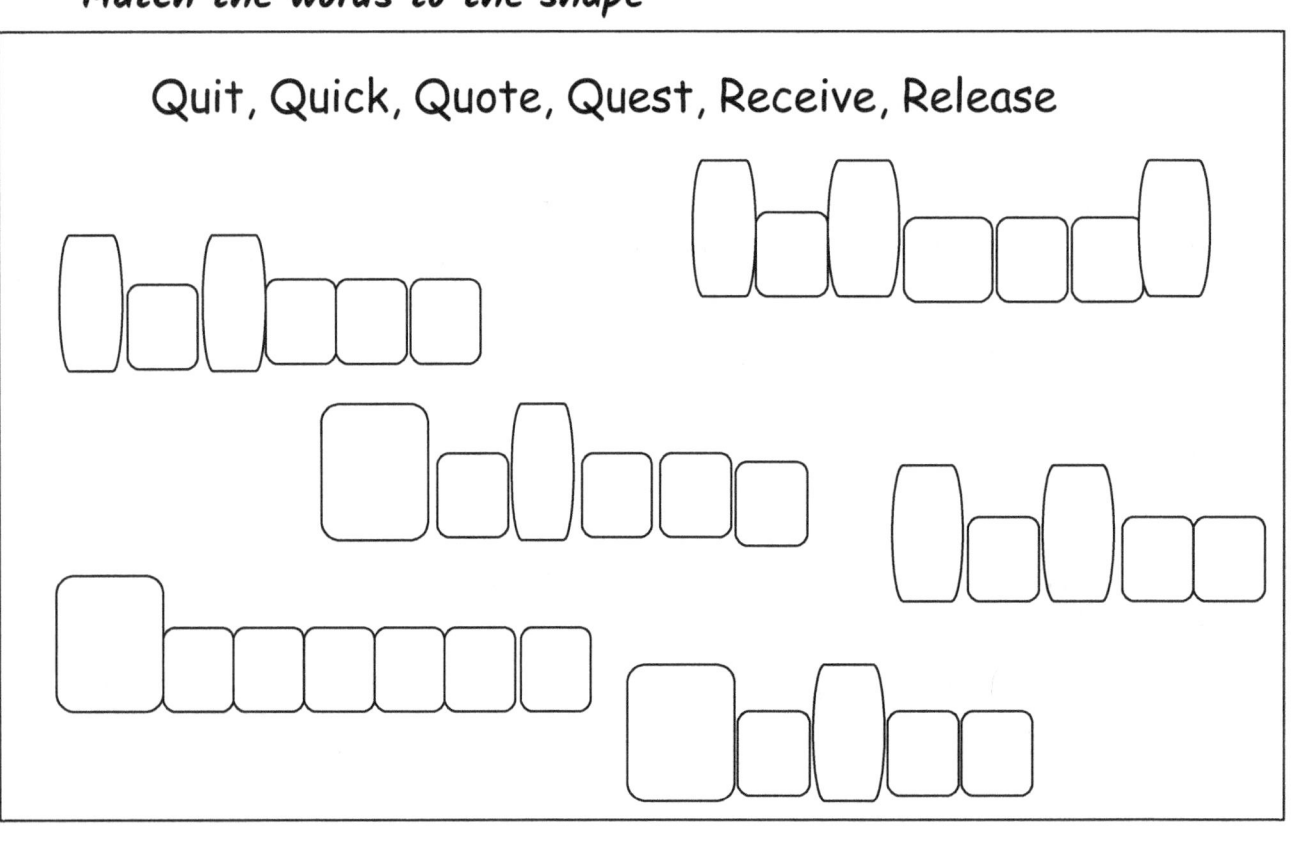

Wordsearch

Lesson # 14

M	Q	R	B	Q	L	Z	V	E	P	T	J	Q	S	Q
I	E	Q	B	I	G	K	J	C	C	V	M	Y	D	C
K	V	H	Z	O	C	J	I	D	T	K	I	Q	L	F
Y	O	N	D	I	Y	D	P	H	G	Z	I	Q	E	R
D	Y	H	U	K	R	N	O	P	V	S	G	P	K	U
C	I	Q	L	H	V	D	S	Z	Q	U	Q	U	O	T
R	P	M	R	F	A	U	P	J	V	U	C	U	I	R
P	F	S	E	M	X	W	V	U	W	S	I	Z	J	Q
G	N	E	C	O	U	B	I	Y	P	O	I	T	Z	M
X	L	V	E	C	P	J	S	Z	E	Y	Q	S	Z	U
N	P	I	I	U	Q	C	M	S	T	Q	H	F	V	I
J	N	O	V	Q	A	E	A	B	L	F	G	P	R	U
Y	P	K	E	D	U	E	Q	S	E	N	P	K	S	V
O	R	E	B	A	L	E	R	B	E	D	T	B	F	A
U	O	C	Z	E	I	B	S	X	V	V	O	D	V	B
U	X	D	R	J	E	C	U	T	X	E	D	I	B	W

QUEST   QUICK
QUIT   QUOTE
RECEIVE   RELEASE

Lesson 15

Re-write Words

Recipe			
Recipient			
Remote			
Remove			
Secret			
Secretary			

Find Letters

Recipe	M r o p e n m d c r g j i a p e k t w p i z x o p l n
Recipient	g r o j e b m q u c b i p i t s r e l g o j a n u t r n
Remote	z w m r i e k a n h d s m u e o b r m k d a j t e p
Remove	L k j i r l n d e r s l k g m q o t d i x y o v h g l e t
Secret	A s d l e d g i c l p t r n g h e n q x e t h r c j k t
Secretary	B p s r m k l e p n c f j t d r h e d t f a d l r p y b

These mnemonics are designed to create memorable associations or phrases that can help you remember the words better. Feel free to modify them or come up with your own mnemonics based on what helps you remember most effectively!

Recipe:
Mnemonic: "Remember Every Cooking Process, It's Creative and Enjoyable."

Recipient:
Mnemonic: "Receiving Envelopes, Cards, In Presents, It's Exciting, Notable, and Treasured."

Remote:
Mnemonic: "Relaxing Environment, Makes One Think Effectively."

Remove:
Mnemonic: "Remove Every Messy Object, Very Efficiently."

Secret:
Mnemonic: "Sharing Every Concern Ruins Essential Trust."

Secretary:
Mnemonic: "Skilled Employee Cares for Recording Important Tasks, Answering Responsibilities Year-round."

Find Meanings from Dictionary and write them here

Recipe _____

Recipient _____

Remote _____

Remove _____

Secret _____

Secretary _____

Write out these words in Capital letters

recipe _____

recipient _____

remote _____

remove _____

secret _____

secretary _____

Write out the Synonyms and Antonyms of these words

	Synonyms	Antonyms
Recipe		
Recipient		
Remote		
Remove		
Secret		
Secretary		

Match the Unscramble Words

Recipe	rveeom	....
Recipient	tmereo	....
Remote	teiprneci	....
Remove	cireep	....
Secret	sreect	....
Secretary	sarrecyet	....

Make the sentences by using given words

Recipe _____

Recipient _____

Remote _____

Remove _____

Secret _____

Secretary _____

Match the words to the shape

Recipe, Recipient, Remote, Remove, Secret, Secretary

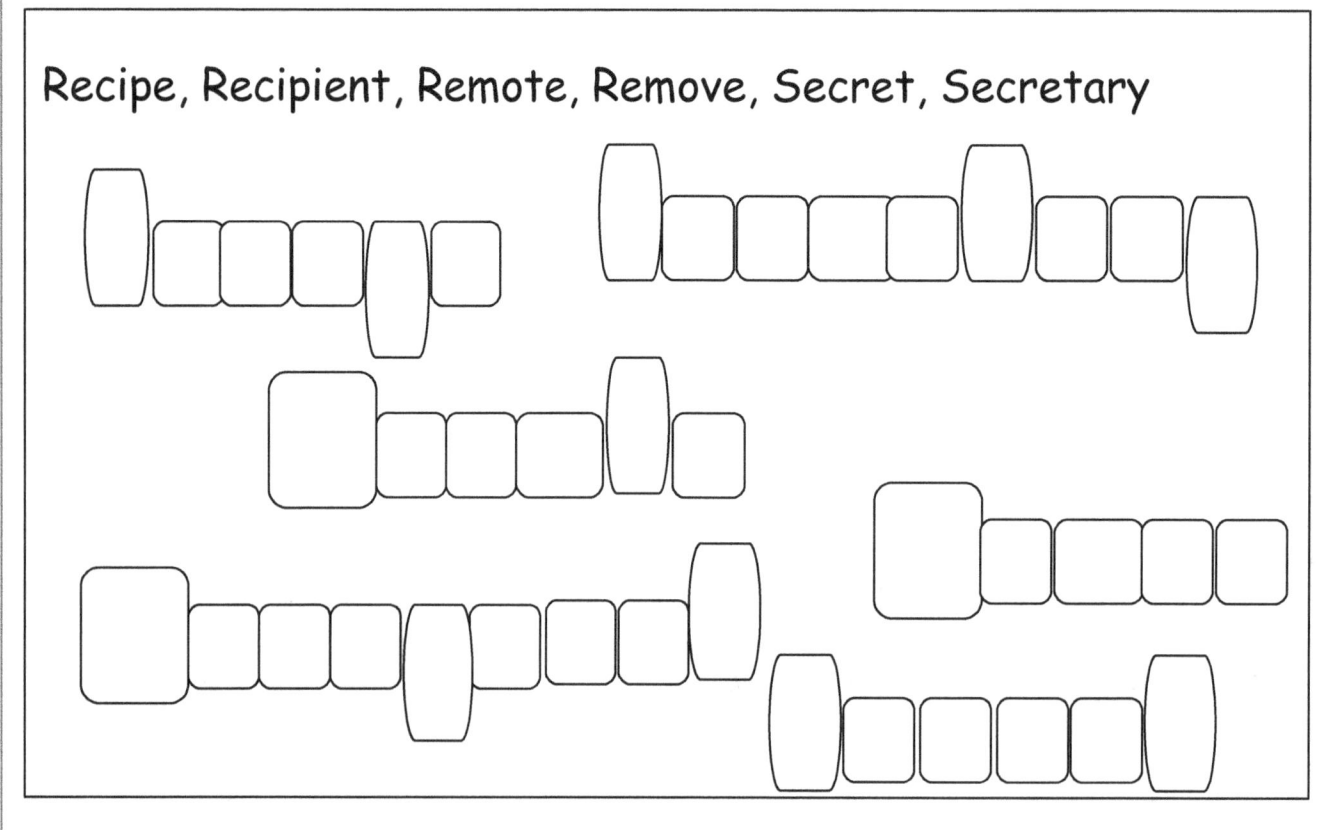

Across

4. An administrative professional who assists with various tasks and manages correspondence.
5. The person or entity that receives something.
6. To take something away or eliminate it.

Down

1. Something kept hidden or not known by others.
2. A device used to control electronic equipment from a distance.
3. A set of instructions for preparing a particular dish.

Fill the blanks by using words you have learned in this passage

A well-crafted _____ is like a treasure map, guiding chefs on a culinary adventure. It provides the necessary steps and ingredients to transform raw elements into gastronomic delights. From beginners following a simple recipe to experienced cooks experimenting with their own creations, the art of cooking begins with a carefully written _____.

In today's digital age, technology has brought the world of recipes within _____ reach. With a few clicks, cooks can explore a vast collection of culinary inspirations from all corners of the globe. Whether it's discovering exotic flavors or revisiting timeless classics, the _____ convenience of accessing recipes online has revolutionized the way we approach cooking.

One essential step in any recipe is to _____ any unwanted elements. Whether it's peeling vegetables, discarding seeds, or trimming excess fat, the process of _____ ensures that the final dish is refined and perfected. This meticulous attention to detail allows the true flavors and textures to shine, making every bite a culinary pleasure.

However, nestled within the instructions of a recipe, there may be a _____ ingredient. This _____ ingredient is the key to unlocking extraordinary flavors, known only to the creator. Passed down through generations or discovered through countless trials, this secret imparts a special touch that elevates the dish to new heights.

In the end, a well-crafted recipe has the power to transform ingredients into memorable experiences. The _____ of such culinary creations eagerly anticipates the final result. Guided by the recipe and entrusted with the _____ ingredient, the chef becomes a culinary _____, orchestrating a symphony of flavors that delights the palate and nourishes the soul.

Wordsearch

Lesson #15

```
U R T F P A T M D V R V X B G I
X U V Q M P D Y W J U O G F Z F
R E F N F P E J Y A Q C H M O U
R O K S N H Q G D T A U D V A G
I Q B S J M C T E W P Q E Y Q T
I C D W I D D T R L G P H U X P
H E Z P E B O M P Z I R R N A O
W P M B R M S R E C C E J Q Q V
F K U L E P E D E Z P C K D P I
V N S R M X C R H M N I Q G F S
F A H H O I R Z N J U P E V S S
Z S Q B V C E J O N E I I H D S
B Z C G E Q T C S B Q E F D U T
Q C G B D P X F O H Z N T C K S
U D D Y U G C X P R L T X Q J R
V L A X W S E C R E T A R Y Z W
```

RECIPE   RECIPIENT
REMOTE   REMOVE
SECRET   SECRETARY

Lesson 16

Re-write Words

Several			
Severe			
Sentiment			
Sensitive			
Tender			
Trend			

Find Letters

Several	M g o p s n e d h v g e j r a p e k t w p l z x o p
Severe	g r s j n b m q u e b p v t s e w l g o j a r u k r
Sentiment	s w m p i e k a n h t s i r m e c b r n k d a j t e
Sensitive	L k j i a s e n d m r s l i g o q w t d i x y v h g e
Tender	A b t l c d g e o l p t s n g h r d q x e f h r c j k
Trend	B p s r m k t q p r e f j t d n h a d r t f d l e p w

These mnemonics are designed to create memorable associations or phrases that can help you remember the words better. Feel free to modify them or come up with your own mnemonics based on what helps you remember most effectively!

Several:
Mnemonic: "Some Eggs Varying, Embellish Refined Almonds, Lavender."

Severe:
Mnemonic: "Sharp Edge, Very Extreme, Requires Emergency."

Sentiment:
Mnemonic: "Soothing Emotions, Nostalgia, Touching Moments In Every Note."

Sensitive:
Mnemonic: "Softly Engaging, Needs Sensible Input, Vibrates Intricately To Emotions."

Tender:
Mnemonic: "Touching, Embracing, Nurturing, Demonstrates Endless Respect."

Trend:
Mnemonic: "Tastes Really Exciting, New, and Daring."

Find Meanings from Dictionary and write them here

Several _____

Severe _____

Sentiment _____

Sensitive _____

Tender _____

Trend _____

Write out these words in Capital letters

several _____

severe _____

sentiment _____

sensitive _____

tender _____

trend _____

Find hidden words

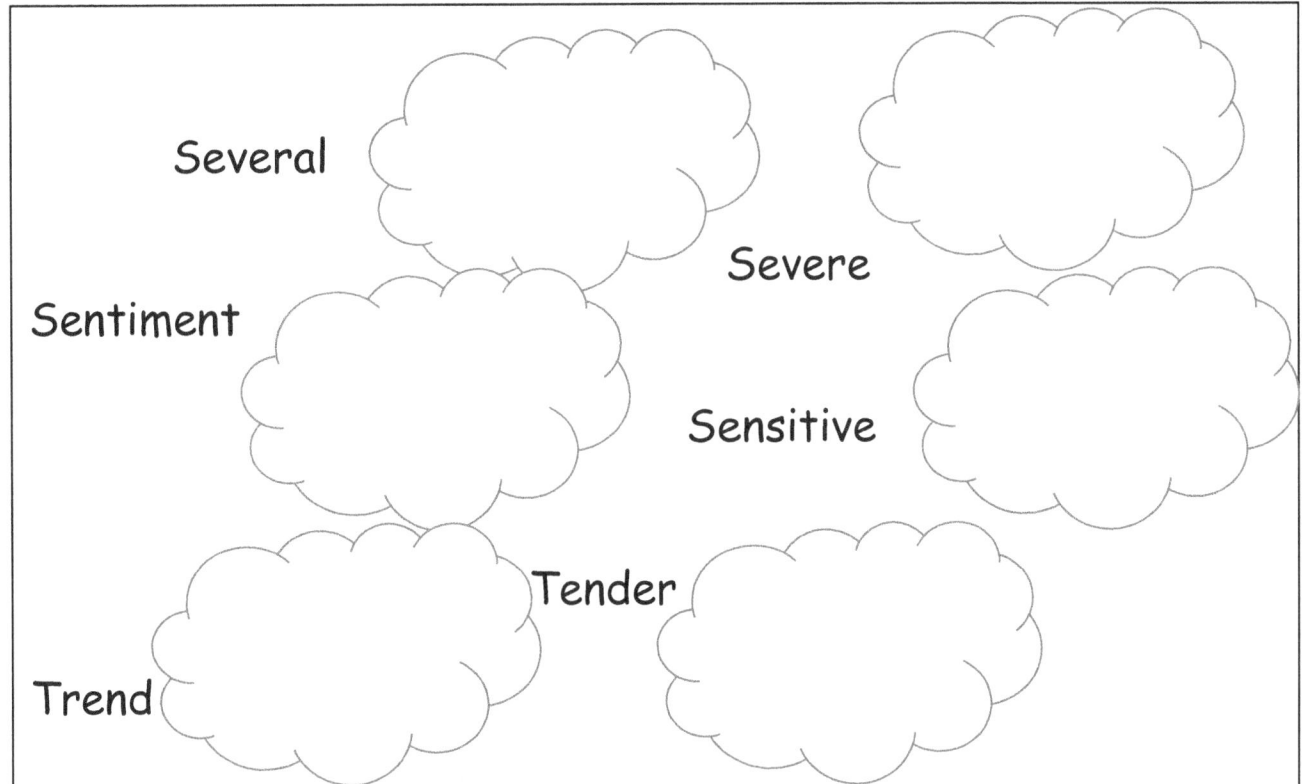

Several

Sentiment

Severe

Sensitive

Tender

Trend

Match the Unscramble Words

Several	niettemns	....
Severe	srleeav	....
Sentiment	rtndee	....
Sensitive	veseer	....
Tender	rdtne	....
Trend	vieseinst	....

Lesson #16

```
B M O E A A I V Z O E R C G N P
W K M L X D S E N S I T I V E E
Q R W T N K K M C W C Q O U T H
C K T E K L M N K F U L R D V Q
X R E O S Z Z S B Y A S X U E A
D M N J E W L R G Q I I W E T D
I R D X N X X S K Q Z I Q Z O E
D S E K T W R E Z L V S J G R N
V D R Z I Z I V H N P E V E D K
W T X I M N V E V R O O V N W N
F H B F E J C R I U V E E W E Z
K O X E N E K A E C S R K F L H
X R E Z T S H L A H T L X V L U
E J W D E W Z G G R E I I M O K
D R Z S M P A W L L H N Y B V Y
C Z W B A W M R V T F F R U U Q
```

SENSITIVE
SEVERAL
TENDER

SENTIMENT
SEVERE
TREND

Read the passage & Underline the words you have learned in this lesson

In recent years, there has been a significant shift in societal dynamics, marked by several noteworthy trends. One such trend revolves around a growing sentiment of compassion and empathy towards sensitive and tender issues. People are becoming more aware of the severe impact that certain actions and words can have on others, leading to a heightened sense of sensitivity and understanding. This trend is indicative of a collective desire to foster a more inclusive and caring environment, where individuals actively engage in acts of kindness and consideration. It is heartening to witness the transformational power of such sentiments, as they contribute to the overall well-being of society and create spaces where vulnerable populations can feel supported and valued. This shift towards empathy and tenderness reflects a positive trajectory, signaling a societal evolution that embraces the diversity of human experiences and champions emotional intelligence as an essential aspect of human interaction.

Match the words to the shape

Several, Severe, Sentiment, Sensitive, Tender, Trend

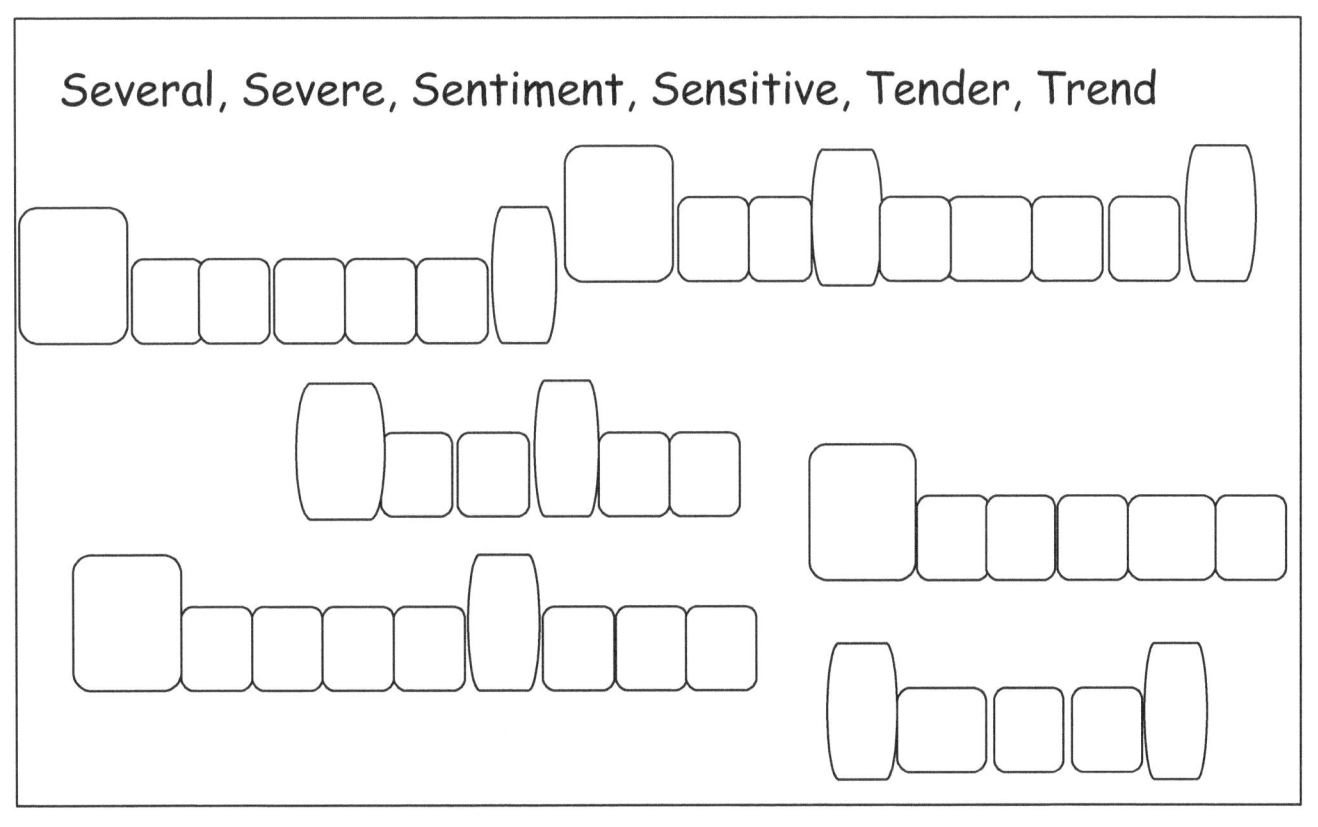

Across

4. More than a few, but not many.
5. A general direction in which something is developing or changing.
6. Easily affected or influenced, often referring to one's feelings or emotions.

Down

1. A personal feeling or emotion towards something or someone.
2. Extremely intense or serious.
3. Gentle, delicate, or easily damaged.

Lesson 17

Re-write Words

Thread			
Threat			
Thrive			
Thrown			
Unique			
Unite			

Find Letters

Thread	M g t p s h m d h r g j e a p e k d w p i z x o p l
Threat	g r o j n t m q h e b p r t s r a l g o j a t u k r n
Thrive	z t m p i h k a r h d s i u e c b v m k d a j t e p
Thrown	L k j i a t h n d m r s l k g o q w t d i x y n h g l
Unique	A u d l n d g i o l p t s n q h r u q x e f h r c j k
Unite	B p s r u k l q p n e f j i d s h a d r t f d l e p w b

These mnemonics are designed to create memorable associations or phrases that can help you remember the words better. Feel free to modify them or come up with your own mnemonics based on what helps you remember most effectively!

Thread:
Mnemonic: "Thin, Helpful, and Reliable, Essential for All Dresses."

Threat:
Mnemonic: "This Hostile Rabbit Emerged, A Terrifying situation!"

Thrive:
Mnemonic: "To Have Real Inspirations, Value Effort."

Thrown:
Mnemonic: "Tossed Heavily, Resulting in Overwhelming Nuisance."

Unique:
Mnemonic: "Unicorns Never Imitate, Quirky, Unmatched, Extraordinary."

Unite:
Mnemonic: "Us, Neighbors, In The Endeavor, Together, Emerge."

Find Meanings from Dictionary and write them here

Thread _____

Threat _____

Thrive _____

Thrown _____

Unique _____

Unite _____

Write out these words in Capital letters

thread _____

threat _____

thrive _____

thrown _____

unique _____

unite _____

Here are mnemonic examples: read them and try to make your own

Thread: "Tightly Holding Rope's End And Dressing" - Imagine a mnemonic where you associate the word "Thread" with the phrase "Tightly Holding Rope's End And Dressing" to remember its meaning related to sewing or connecting things together.

Threat: "Taking Heed, React Early And Take precautions" - Create a mnemonic where "Threat" is associated with the phrase "Taking Heed, React Early And Take precautions" to remind yourself to be cautious and take action when facing potential dangers.

Thrive: "Taking Huge Risks Inspires Victories and Excitement" - Associate the word "Thrive" with the phrase "Taking Huge Risks Inspires Victories and Excitement" to remind yourself of the positive outcomes that can be achieved by embracing challenges and stepping out of your comfort zone.

Thrown: "Throwing Hard, Remember Only Where it Lands Now" - Create a mnemonic where "Thrown" is associated with the phrase "Throwing Hard, Remember Only Where it Lands Now" to help remember the action of throwing something forcefully.

Unique: "Unforgettable and Never Identical, Quite Extraordinary" - Associate the word "Unique" with the phrase "Unforgettable and Never Identical, Quite Extraordinary" to emphasize its meaning of being one-of-a-kind or distinct from others.

Unite: "Uniting Nations, Inspiring Togetherness and Empathy" - Create a mnemonic where "Unite" is associated with the phrase "Uniting Nations, Inspiring Togetherness and Empathy" to highlight its meaning of bringing people together and fostering harmony.

Identify & Underline the Synonyms and Antonyms of words you have learned

- The two organizations decided to merge, pooling their resources and expertise.
- The conflicting opinions served only to further divide the already fragmented group.
- Her style was distinct, setting her apart from others in the fashion industry.
- The mundane design made it blend in with the common furniture in the room.
- Despite the challenges, the business managed to flourish and expand.
- The company continued to struggle, facing financial difficulties.
- He angrily hurled the object across the room, venting his frustration.
- The agile goalkeeper effortlessly caught the ball, preventing a goal.

Match the Unscramble Words

Thread	trnwho	....
Threat	trvieh	....
Thrive	drthae	....
Thrown	niuequ	....
Unique	tunie	....
Unite	hertat	....

Fill the blanks and Make the sentences using above words

1. Her artistic style was truly _____, capturing attention with its originality and creativity.

2. The citizens came together to _____ for a common cause, rallying behind a shared goal.

3. Despite facing numerous challenges, the small business managed to _____ and achieve success.

4. In a fit of anger, he _____ the book across the room, scattering pages everywhere.

5. The tailor carefully sewed the _____ through the fabric, creating intricate patterns.

6. The menacing _____ of violence hung over the town, causing fear among its residents.

Match the words to the shape

Thread, Threat, Thrive, Thrown, Unique, Unite

Wordsearch

Lesson #17

R	G	B	N	D	I	X	R	H	Q	R	L	A	A	I	Z
X	N	W	U	S	X	U	F	P	X	D	J	D	D	G	K
M	R	C	V	Z	D	A	N	Q	T	Q	M	O	C	K	R
J	U	F	W	Q	T	O	A	I	K	Y	U	T	F	W	G
V	R	Z	H	Y	X	Z	T	T	Q	T	H	H	X	A	U
T	M	C	J	U	Z	Q	W	H	V	U	Q	R	Z	U	W
Z	G	Q	T	V	O	E	T	U	R	E	E	I	V	Y	L
E	F	J	L	W	U	T	Y	U	V	O	C	V	O	M	M
P	Y	C	M	O	I	N	H	E	W	E	W	E	J	O	U
V	K	N	A	B	K	K	I	R	Y	W	S	N	Y	W	C
O	E	S	P	C	G	Y	P	T	E	L	G	E	Y	X	H
W	S	F	I	X	A	O	Z	O	E	A	A	H	Y	B	K
Y	I	M	P	B	A	Y	S	D	Q	D	D	U	M	Y	H
C	D	D	I	V	Q	N	P	B	Q	X	S	R	U	N	W
O	F	U	H	P	T	H	R	E	A	T	V	H	N	K	H
E	K	Q	H	B	B	Z	K	P	Z	W	I	H	F	L	D

THREAD THREAT
THRIVE THROWN
UNIQUE UNITE

What rhymes with these words

Thread

Threat

Thrive

Thrown

Unique

Unite

Find hidden words

Thread

Threat

Thrive

Thrown

Unique

Unite

Across

2. To bring together or join into a single entity or group.
4. A thin strand used in sewing or weaving.
6. To grow, develop, or prosper vigorously.

Down

1. One of a kind; unparalleled or distinct from others.
3. A potential danger or source of harm.
5. Past participle of "throw," meaning to propel or fling something through the air.

Lesson 18

Re-write Words

User			
Usual			
Unfair			
Unfold			
Variety			
Various			

Find Letters

User	M u o p s n m d h e g j r a p e k t w p i z x o p l n
Usual	g r o j u b m s q u e b p v t a r w l g o j a r u k r
Unfair	z w m p u e k a n h d s f u e a b r m k i a j t r e p
Unfold	L u j i a l n d m r s f k g o q w l d i x y o h g l n t
Variety	A v d l c d g a o l p r s n g h i n q x e f t r c y k t
Various	B p s r m v l q p n a f j t d r h i d o t f d l u p s b

These mnemonics are designed to create memorable associations or phrases that can help you remember the words better. Feel free to modify them or come up with your own mnemonics based on what helps you remember most effectively!

User:
Mnemonic: "Using Some Electronic Resources."

Usual:
Mnemonic: "Usually, Similar And Regular."

Unfair:
Mnemonic: "Unjust, Not Acceptable, I Refuse."

Unfold:
Mnemonic: "Unveil New Facts, Open Lucid Details."

Variety:
Mnemonic: "Various Array, Rich In Tastes, Yummy!"

Various:
Mnemonic: "Varying And Random, I Observe Unique Sights."

Find Meanings from Dictionary and write them here

User _____

Usual _____

Unfair _____

Unfold _____

Variety _____

Various _____

Write out these words in Capital letters

user _____

usual _____

unfair _____

unfold _____

variety _____

various _____

Write out the Synonyms and Antonyms of these words

	Synonyms	Antonyms
User		
Usual		
Unfair		
Unfold		
Variety		
Various		

Match the Unscramble Words

User	ruasovi	....
Usual	tiarvye	....
Unfair	ndulof	....
Unfold	ruse	....
Variety	ulsau	....
Various	nifaru	....

Across

2. Not just or equitable; biased or unjust.
3. An individual who interacts with or utilizes a system, platform, or device.
4. Referring to multiple or different kinds, types, or options.
5. To open up, reveal, or develop gradually.

Down

1. A diverse range or assortment of different types or kinds.
3. Something that is customary, typical, or frequently occurring.

Fill the blanks and Make the sentences using above words

1. Let me _____ the story for you, revealing the hidden twists and turns that will captivate your imagination.

2. The store offers a wide _____ of products, catering to the diverse preferences of its customers.

3. The workshop covered _____ topics, ranging from basic computer skills to advanced programming techniques.

4. As a website, we strive to provide an exceptional experience for every _____ who visits our platform.

5. It was a _____ day at the office, with everyone going about their _____ tasks and responsibilities.

6. The judge's decision was deemed _____ by the defendant, as they felt they hadn't received a fair trial.

Match the words to the shape

User, Usual, Unfair, Unfold, Variety, Various

Wordsearch

Lesson #18

T	G	W	O	X	Q	P	H	D	V	N	K	B	R	S	T
C	W	Y	B	M	V	E	R	S	D	U	O	Q	N	U	Q
R	U	P	E	B	G	A	Y	Y	W	S	S	W	M	W	Y
C	N	T	M	K	J	Q	R	B	R	E	T	P	A	U	F
G	F	W	M	F	W	M	L	I	M	R	D	E	B	A	X
T	A	F	O	D	O	A	K	C	O	Y	F	B	M	L	G
A	I	L	H	J	C	T	T	V	A	U	C	J	E	H	W
M	R	J	Z	F	L	A	Y	U	J	X	S	J	B	X	T
I	C	U	T	L	E	F	Z	I	D	G	H	V	P	V	M
E	E	I	N	V	S	C	N	M	S	Z	D	A	J	U	C
T	W	T	K	F	Y	L	A	F	F	U	V	R	R	N	D
R	L	F	V	M	O	V	P	P	C	S	N	I	A	U	T
K	J	A	O	K	I	L	X	T	H	U	X	E	M	Y	B
Z	L	V	W	N	D	K	D	J	Q	A	D	T	T	U	A
Q	G	M	R	M	E	E	C	X	G	L	Z	Y	T	U	W
S	X	W	H	A	B	W	S	R	S	D	O	T	O	E	R

UNFAIR UNFOLD
USER USUAL
VARIETY VARIOUS

Lesson 19

Re-write Words

Vendor			
Venture			
Verdict			
Version			
Violent			
Virtual			

Find Letters

Vendor	M v o p s e m d h r g j n a p d k t o p i z r o p l n
Venture	g r o j v b m e u n b p v t s r u l g o j a r u e k r n
Verdict	z v m p i e k a r h d s u e i c b r m k d a j t e p m
Version	L k j i a v n e m r s l k g i q w t d x y o h g l n t p
Violent	A v d l c d g i o l p s e g h r n q x e f h r c j k t m
Virtual	B p s r m v l q i n e f j t d r h a t r u f d a l p w b o

These mnemonics are designed to create memorable associations or phrases that can help you remember the words better. Feel free to modify them or come up with your own mnemonics based on what helps you remember most effectively!

Vendor:
Mnemonic: "Very Efficient Negotiator, Delivers Outstanding Resources."

Venture:
Mnemonic: "Venturing into Exciting New Territories, Uplifting Business Enterprises."

Verdict:
Mnemonic: "Very Evident Ruling, Clearly Decided, Taking."

Version:
Mnemonic: "Variations Emerge, Resulting in Several Interpretations, Outstandingly Noteworthy."

Violent:
Mnemonic: "Very Intense, Outburst, Lacking Empathy, Notable Threat."

Virtual:
Mnemonic: "Vivid, Imaginary Reality, Ultimately Affects Life."

Find Meanings from Dictionary and write them here

Vendor _____

Venture _____

Verdict _____

Version _____

Violent _____

Virtual _____

Write out these words in Capital letters

vendor _____

venture _____

verdict _____

version _____

violent _____

virtual _____

Across
1. A person or entity that sells goods or services.
3. An undertaking or business enterprise involving risk, especially a new and innovative one.
4. Existing or occurring through digital or simulated means, rather than in a physical form or space.
5. Involving or characterized by physical force or aggression.

Down
1. The formal decision or judgment made by a jury or judge at the end of a trial.
2. A particular form or variant of something, often referring to a revised or updated edition.

Write out the Synonyms and Antonyms of these words

	Synonyms	Antonyms
Vendor		
Venture		
Verdict		
Version		
Violent		
Virtual		

Match the Unscramble Words

Vendor	vcedtri	....
Venture	tiaruvl	....
Verdict	tvlenio	....
Version	nseoriv	....
Violent	ndorev	....
Virtual	teveurn	....

Read the passage carefully, fill in the blanks with above words, and then answer the accompanying questions.

In the bustling market square, a _____ set up a colorful stall, showcasing an enticing array of handmade crafts and unique artifacts. As shoppers perused the offerings, the vendor skillfully explained the stories behind each item, adding to the charm of the experience. This entrepreneurial _____ represented a brave step for the vendor, who had embarked on a new business endeavor to share their artistic creations with the world.

Meanwhile, in a courtroom drama that had captured the nation's attention, the jury delivered a surprising _____. The _____ came after weeks of intense deliberation, and its impact reverberated throughout society. The verdict held the power to reshape the lives of the individuals involved and even influenced public opinion on matters of justice and equality.

In the realm of technology, the latest _____ of a popular software application was eagerly anticipated. Users were excitedly waiting for the new _____, which promised enhanced functionality and a more intuitive user interface. The software company worked diligently to address bugs and incorporate user feedback, ensuring that the latest version would meet the expectations of their loyal customer base.

Unfortunately, the evening news recounted yet another _____ incident, emphasizing the need for community action against such acts of harm. It served as a stark reminder of the importance of addressing the root causes of violence and working collectively to foster safer and more inclusive environments.

Moreover, as technology advanced, people found themselves increasingly immersed in _____ realms. Virtual reality platforms offered immersive experiences, where users could explore virtual landscapes, attend virtual concerts, or engage in virtual social interactions. This shift toward the _____ realm transformed the way individuals connected and experienced the world around them.

Please answer the following questions based on the provided reading comprehension passage.

1. What was the vendor showcasing at the colorful stall?

2. Why was the vendor's business considered a venture?

3. What did the jury deliver after weeks of deliberation?

4. What were users eagerly awaiting in the realm of technology?

5. How did virtual reality platforms impact people's experiences?

Match the words to the shape

Vendor, Venture, Verdict, Version, Violent, Virtual

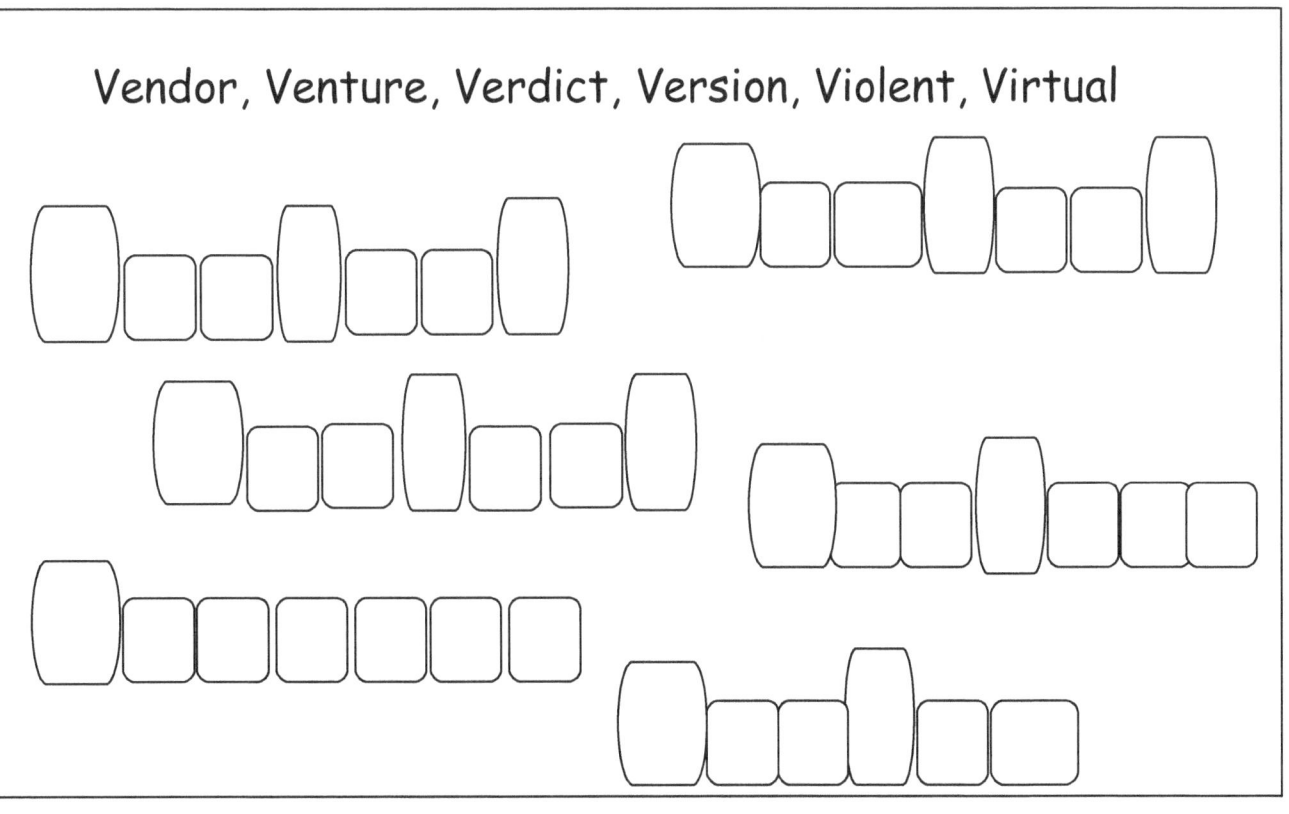

Wordsearch

Lesson #19

F	J	Z	Q	B	Y	N	R	T	D	W	A	Z	W	K	O
Q	H	V	N	X	S	I	A	K	Y	V	W	Y	J	J	B
J	V	M	I	K	E	D	Q	T	D	I	D	Z	L	G	R
R	E	G	Z	R	C	D	H	K	W	R	J	N	Z	E	Y
Q	N	C	X	W	A	W	A	N	W	T	X	B	K	Z	D
Y	T	Q	G	G	I	M	V	Y	R	U	A	E	O	O	P
L	U	Y	Y	E	T	H	Y	Z	A	A	D	E	V	H	Y
Y	R	B	X	I	E	U	P	N	E	L	E	D	V	T	U
M	E	H	R	Z	R	I	O	J	J	R	E	U	Z	Z	P
S	F	H	T	S	W	I	M	M	A	B	C	H	T	U	F
W	S	D	K	H	S	W	C	Y	M	Q	U	R	T	Y	V
M	H	G	U	R	N	Z	V	I	O	L	E	N	T	J	Z
E	Q	N	E	M	K	M	X	C	Y	C	H	U	Q	B	R
J	I	V	E	R	D	I	C	T	H	S	K	B	Y	P	L
R	P	S	S	V	P	D	V	E	N	D	O	R	U	K	C
I	U	K	X	B	V	H	Y	I	L	N	B	B	E	V	S

VENDOR   VENTURE
VERDICT   VERSION
VIOLENT   VIRTUAL

What rhymes with these words

Vendor, Venture, Verdict, Version, Violent, Virtual

Find hidden words

Vendor, Venture, Verdict, Version, Violent, Virtual

Lesson 20

Re-write Words

Want			
Wander			
Wonder			
Worry			
Worth			
Wound			

Find Letters

Want	M g w p s m d h r g j r a p e n k t w p i z x o p l
Wander	g r o j w b m q u a b p v t n r w d g o j e r u k r
Wonder	z w m p i o k a n h d s u e c b r m k d a j t e p n
Worry	L k j i a l w d m s l k g o q r t d i r y o h y l n t m
Worth	A w d l c d g i o l p t s n g r n q x e f t h r c j k
Wound	B p s r w k l q p o e f j u t d n h a d r t f d l e p

These mnemonics are designed to create memorable associations or phrases that can help you remember the words better. Feel free to modify them or come up with your own mnemonics based on what helps you remember most effectively!

Want:
Mnemonic: "Wishing And Needing Things."

Wander:
Mnemonic: "Walking And Navigating, Discovering Endless Roads."

Wonder:
Mnemonic: "Wishing On New Dreams, Expecting Remarkable."

Worry:
Mnemonic: "Wasting Our Restless Thoughts, Regretfully Yearning."

Worth:
Mnemonic: "Weighing Our Resources, Their Value."

Wound:
Mnemonic: "With Ouch, Understanding No Delight."

Find Meanings from Dictionary and write them here

Want _____

Wander _____

Wonder _____

Worry _____

Worth _____

Wound _____

Write out these words in Capital letters

want _____

wander _____

wonder _____

worry _____

worth _____

wound _____

Write out the Synonyms and Antonyms of these words

	Synonyms	Antonyms
Want		
Wander		
Wonder		
Worry		
Worth		
Wound		

Match the Unscramble Words

Want	dnwuo	....
Wander	dnerow	....
Wonder	rotwh	....
Worry	nwta	....
Worth	ryowr	....
Wound	deranw	....

Across

1. To feel anxious or concerned about something.
2. To desire or wish for something.
3. To roam or explore aimlessly or without a specific destination.

Down

1. An injury, typically involving a break in the skin or flesh.
2. The value or importance of something.
3. To feel curiosity or amazement about something.

Fill in the blanks with the words you have learned in this lesson

In life's journey, we often _____, seeking new experiences and adventures. We _____ through the world, curious about its mysteries and possibilities. Along the way, we may _____ about the future, concerned about what lies ahead. Yet, amidst the uncertainties, it is important to remember that every step we take is _____ taking. Despite the occasional _____ we may encounter, the beauty of the journey is in the lessons learned and the growth experienced.

Match the words to the shape

Want, Wander, Wonder, Worry, Worth, Wound

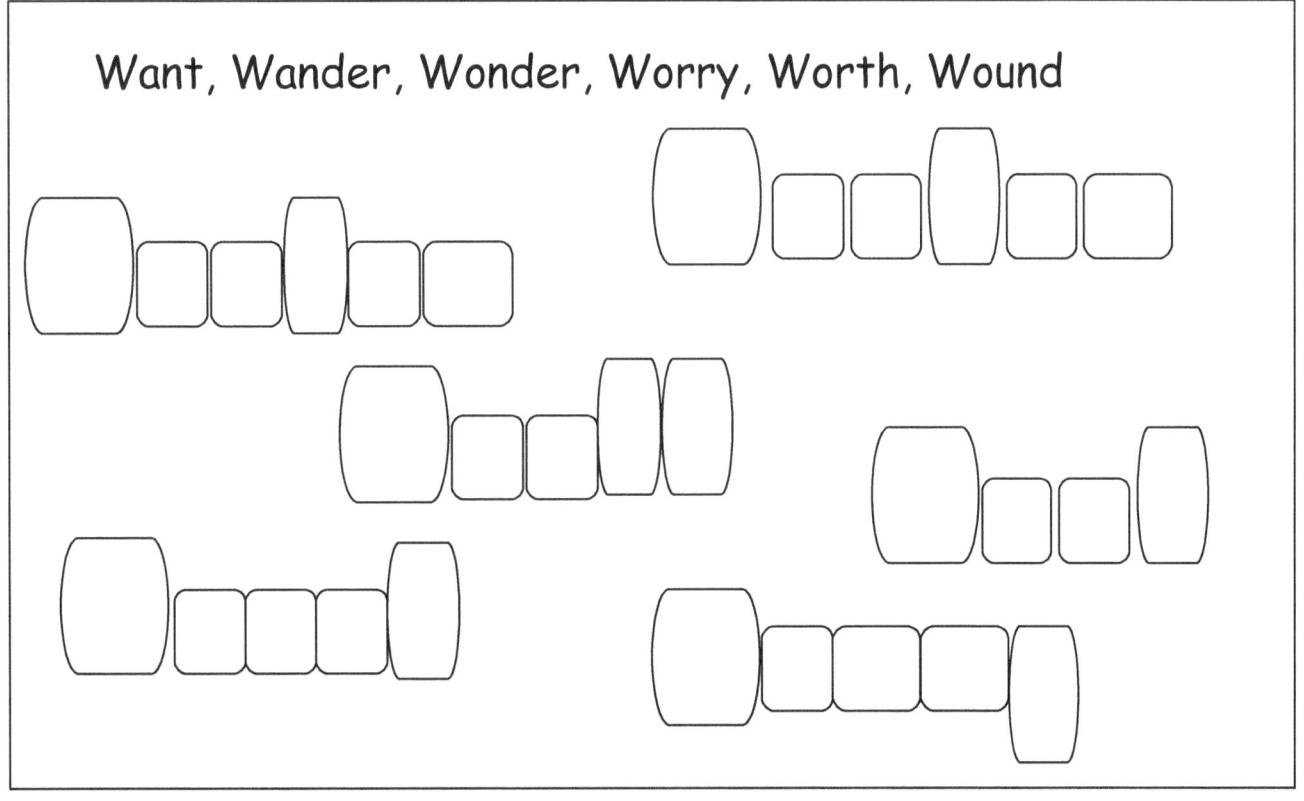

Wordsearch

Lesson #20

A	D	M	R	V	A	U	V	U	C	F	P	P	W	F	P
C	O	U	M	X	M	O	W	O	U	N	D	A	R	E	R
F	M	R	Q	V	J	U	J	X	Z	J	E	F	R	T	B
J	M	W	O	T	W	H	S	P	K	H	B	J	S	J	J
Z	K	T	N	X	O	T	B	J	T	W	O	N	D	E	R
F	X	A	H	H	C	I	X	Q	V	O	L	X	Q	I	R
O	W	O	C	I	W	M	K	W	M	N	L	B	G	N	P
S	L	Q	E	G	H	M	B	K	C	N	V	B	C	V	H
W	N	R	K	I	K	V	C	J	W	N	G	O	F	S
S	H	F	M	H	B	I	M	S	V	B	O	C	X	Q	I
T	Y	P	K	Y	W	I	Z	K	Z	N	W	R	Y	G	Q
I	T	I	I	R	U	U	J	W	O	R	T	H	R	Y	F
B	T	A	X	K	X	V	G	V	J	L	E	P	I	Y	D
D	U	D	H	O	Y	Z	T	A	N	P	M	D	Q	N	Z
U	Q	I	E	F	B	Z	B	I	W	A	N	D	E	R	O
J	G	Z	U	T	P	Q	D	O	Y	M	A	S	H	M	F

WANDER   WANT
WONDER   WORRY
WORTH   WOUND

What rhymes with these words

Want Wander, Wonder, Worry, Worth, Wound

Find hidden words

Want Wander, Wonder, Worry, Worth, Wound

Write difficult words and their meanings again

We hope that you enjoyed our efforts in creating this spelling workbook. If possible, we would greatly appreciate it if you could provide a review to help us improve future spelling book series.
Your feedback is valuable to us and will allow us to continue creating helpful resources for children.
Thank you in advance for your time and consideration.

For more Publication; visit our website
www.newbeepublication.com